IN A HEARTBEAT

IN A HEARTBEAT

The Ups and Downs of Life with Atrial Fib

ROSALIE LINVER UNGAR

Boyle
&
Dalton

Book Design & Production
Columbus Publishing Lab
www.ColumbusPublishingLab.com

Paperback ISBN 978-1-63337-112-5
E-book ISBN 978-1-63337-113-2

Printed in the United States of America
1 3 5 7 9 10 8 6 4 2

In memory of my sister,
Madelyn Plaine Wessinger

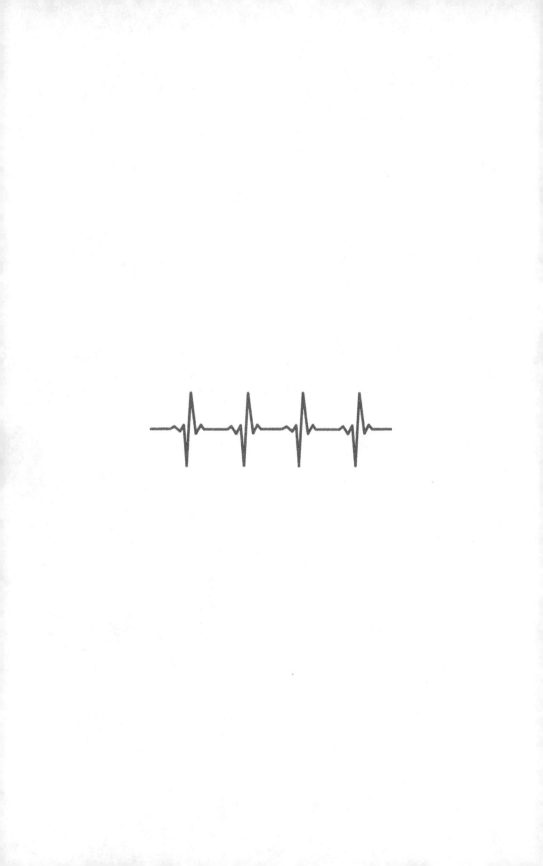

FOREWORD

It is estimated that more than five million adult people in the United States suffer from atrial fibrillation. Thousands more don't know they have it. AF prevalence is projected to increase to twelve million cases by 2030. Brought to my attention recently is the startling information that Google receives, on average, 130,000 inquiries about atrial fibrillation or A-Fib each month.

The A-Fib I've suffered for thirty years was not life-threatening at first. I had unrelated heart and health problems at the same time. None of them are cured. But, they have become manageable through medication, surgical procedures and on-going visits with electrophysiologists, cardiologists, endocrinologists and pharmacologists. And, diet along with exercise were and are my primary regimen for feeling healthy.

Doctors at The Ohio State University Wexner Medical Center in Columbus, Ohio, say that I have reversed any and all heart damage incurred from past heart attacks. This, I am told, is highly unusual. We credit exercise and personal trainers. *In a Heartbeat: The Ups and Downs of Life with Atrial Fib* is my story. I am not a doctor, and my problems may differ from those of others living with the same disease(s). Everyone's body is different and everyone's reaction to medication and procedures may be different.

After years of battling A-Fib and other chronic health issues, I have learned that to know your body and what you put into it is key. Be truthful with your doctors. Ask questions, especially if there's something you don't understand. Learn about the medications you are prescribed and why you are taking them. How will they interact with other meds, food and lifestyle? Be aware of schedules for taking these meds. A friend once told me that she was tired of taking pills, so she decided to take Sundays off and not take any pills on that day. When asking others what medications they take, I've heard replies that they didn't know. The doctor told them to take them, so they do.

On my seventy-fifth birthday my personal trainer had me

do seventy-five push-ups, seventy-five squats, seventy-five crunches with treadmill and spinning bike in between. On my seventy-seventh birthday I did even more than that.

For me, this story is happy and meant to be inspiring. I feel better than I have in over twenty years. I know my limitations and work around them, learning to pay attention to my body, grateful for each day that I do.

CHAPTER ONE
MARCH 2000

Twenty-five men and women hung on my every word. Then I stopped talking, gripped both sides of the podium and looked into their faces while a wrecking ball hit my chest... from the inside.

What seemed like an eternity was only seconds as my first thoughts were: What is this pain? Am I dying? Am I going to pass out? I'm having a heart attack!

My face and neck were on fire. Sweat was starting to pour as I felt my face turning red. This can't be. I'm telling these people how to sell heart-healthy foods! I can't die. It'll pass.

It didn't pass and neither did I. My theatre training taught me that the show must go on, and I lived that rule. Stay vertical and don't panic, I told myself. Exiting the conference room after an abrupt end of my speech, I sat down at a desk in the nearest office where I called my boss, Bob. He was in New Jersey. I was in Omaha, Nebraska.

"I just finished the sales training at the broker's office, and I'm having terrible chest pains," I said, trying not to cry.

"Get to a hospital immediately."

David, the account manager for my product line of Smart Balance food items in Omaha, stood at the door looking nervously at me. "What's happened?" he asked.

"I think I'm having a heart attack and I need to get to the nearest hospital. I don't know where it is, but I need to go now." I didn't even think to call 911, and neither did anyone else. I was the calmest one around.

Quietly I kept telling an imaginary someone, "Please don't let me die. Please don't let me die. My life is good. Please don't let me die in Omaha."

Roger, one of the Omaha salesmen, told David to follow us to the hospital. He would drive me in my rental car. Both men were part of the food brokerage company representing our products in Nebraska, selling them to grocery chains, big and small. I visited their offices three or four times a year to help sell and introduce new items to the line.

The hospital was only minutes away. Mid-morning on a

weekday was slow in the emergency room. I told the first person I saw that I was having a heart attack. David said that he and Roger would be in the waiting room while I was helped onto a gurney and rushed into a room where three doctors joined me and a nurse was ready with IV equipment to start a nitroglycerin drip.

Administration came in to get my medical insurance information. The woman in charge asked me why I didn't call 911 instead of having someone drive me to the hospital. It would have been safer. I told her that it never crossed my mind. Sternly she said to me, "If you ever have another emergency, call nine-one-one."

The pain was still evident but had diminished a little. Blood was drawn. I was sitting up answering questions about my health: Did I have a history of heart problems, were my parents still alive, when did they die, what from, did others in my family have heart problems? Yes. I've had heart problems but only atrial fibrillation for at least twenty years. Maybe longer. I didn't feel it at first. The doctors I dealt with earlier didn't know that much about atrial fibrillation or A-Fib, as it is known. I have a pacemaker. I explained why. And yes, everyone in my family that I knew had died from heart problems. But, always looking for the positive, I said, "No one in my family has had cancer."

At this point I didn't think I was going to die, not now anyway. Actually, except for the gnawing pain in the middle of my chest, I was feeling pretty good. Maybe it was because I was getting so much attention.

The doctors left and returned confirming that I was having a heart attack and that from the blood tests it was evident that I had had another heart episode and smaller heart attack in the past. "Do you recall having this pain on a smaller scale before today?" they asked.

I thought about it. I've had health problems all my life and I try to ignore what I can. "Yes," I said. "Now that I think about it, I had a similar pain at the airport in Columbus on my way to visit my kids in Connecticut."

"When?" one of the doctors asked. He was seated on a swivel chair at a small desk with a box of purple rubber gloves next to a small box of tissues.

"About six weeks ago." I felt stupid. How could I be so naïve about the seriousness of chest pain? "I felt it here," I said, pointing to mid-chest. "I thought a heart attack would be more to the left side. The pain was intense, but it went away after a few minutes."

"On a scale from one to ten, how bad was your pain?" one of the doctors asked. I never liked that question. What did two mean? What did nine mean? I thought I had a high tolerance for pain, so couldn't my two be like someone else's nine?

"Well, I was afraid to get on the plane, but I wanted to see my grandkids. I felt OK, except for being so tired all weekend. Then I recovered, I thought."

What must these doctors think of me? I didn't mean to be blasé, but I did catch some looks of incredulity when I explained that my heart attack occurred while I was speaking to an audience about heart-healthy foods.

"How could I have a heart attack?" I asked. "My cholesterol is checked regularly because I have a cardiologist who monitors my A-Fib. Did this happen because of the A-Fib? I took my pulse in the car on the way to the hospital. It was normal, with the pacemaker at a steady seventy beats per minute. If I were in A-Fib, it would be fast and slow and fluttering and impossible to check. I eat right and I exercise." The doctors looked at me blankly and left the room.

It was time to notify my family. I wouldn't call my children yet. Mark lived in Connecticut and Brian lived in Oregon. First I would call my sister Joan. Then I'd call my boyfriend, Ed. The hospital allowed me to make mobile phone calls in the emergency room, something most hospitals prohibited. I couldn't reach my sister on her cell phone. I vaguely remembered her saying she would be out of town for a meeting somewhere, so I called Ed. He answered, and I immediately told him what had happened and where I was at that moment.

Ed, on a business trip in Washington, D.C., was a passenger in his client's car. They were on the top ramp of a parking garage, ready to descend to an underground level. Another five seconds and I wouldn't have been able to communicate with him either.

Apparently from the expression on his face, his client knew something was wrong and stopped before going down the ramp. "What's the name of the hospital in Omaha?" Ed asked. I didn't know. "Don't worry about it. I'll find Joan and get back to you."

The nurse came in and told me that Bob Harris, my boss, had telephoned and he was talking on the phone to David and Roger still in the waiting room. His message was that he would be in touch and if I was able to call him, do so, but not to worry. He'd find me.

I was still conscious and not feeling badly except for the chest pain that had now changed to an ache. One of the doctors came back with a cardiologist who was usually upstairs, not on the emergency floor. "Your heart attack is still going on. The nitroglycerin is helping. Do you want something to eat?"

"Lordy!" I said, saying a word I never use. "I can't believe any of this is happening. Actually, I am hungry." I sat up on the gurney reaching as far as I could with an IV in my arm. "I never thought a heart attack would go on all day. Is it still doing damage?" I asked.

"We don't know yet. We'll move you upstairs and take some tests." With that the doctors left. An aide came in with a tray of red Jell-O and some broth.

More blood was taken. I wasn't sleepy but was supposed to stay quiet and not move around. As always I had a book in my purse, but couldn't get to it because of the IV in my arm and the monitors recording my every heart movement, pulse, blood pressure and oxygen level. I asked the aide to retrieve my book, *The Poisonwood Bible*, by Barbara Kingsolver. Her novel about the Price daughters from a missionary family in the Belgian Congo got me through the most frightening time of my life.

My bed was moved out of emergency into an elevator and up to the ICU (Intensive Care Unit) where the patient rooms have glass walls and doors that face the center station for nurses, doctors, aides and monitors to keep a constant watch on each and every patient. It was dark outside. Daylight savings time was to begin in a few days, the first Saturday in April. March was almost over and it was looking lamb-like outside. Spring was finally coming to Omaha.

Telephone calls were not allowed the rest of the day. Sleep was fitful. The interruptions were frequent and noisy, leaving me with hours to think and be scared. Nighttime is always worse. Everything is better in daylight.

The new century was not even three months old. Ed and I talked about the millennium, agonizing that in the year 2000 he would be sixty-four and I would turn sixty-three. Aware that we would live to see the new century begin, neither of us ever thought about what would happen after that milestone. Now this. Would my tombstone be carved with beginning and ending dates of 1937–2000?

The next day new cardiologists came in for consultations. Again we went over heart history and the list of medications. My atrial fib had been getting worse. Little progress had been made to correct this chronic condition. Blood thinners and a steady stream of new drugs hitting the market were the only interventions. None agreed with me. Most of them ended with the letters "ide," but they produced side effects of more atrial fib, joint pain or flu-like symptoms. When new drug discoveries were made, I had to check into The Ohio State University Medical Center as an inpatient to be monitored during a three day drug trial. None of these drugs were satisfactory except amiodarone, which worked about ninety percent of the time and carried a list of bizarre side effects.

The ten percent of time that amiodarone didn't work was a doozy. The drug can cause fibrosis of the lungs, liver damage, thyroid problems (which I already had before I started it), blue skin, sensitivity to the sun and deposits on the corneas of the eyes, which often disappear when the drug is stopped. Fortunately, I had none of the more serious side effects, but when the drug wasn't working I had a list from palpitations to shortness of breath and difficulty moving at any pace.

As of day two in Omaha I showed no signs of atrial fib and my blood pressure was normal. "So why the heart attack?" I was convinced that the heart attack had nothing to do with atrial fib. Strange. Both were part of the same organ and were unrelated. Well, why not? The skin's an organ. Does a rash on the arm have anything to do with a bruise on the leg?

The doctors didn't know yet. They needed to do a cardiac catheterization, a procedure where a thin tube is inserted in a blood vessel in the groin and threaded up to the heart to see what is going on. The problem was that the blood thinner medication I was taking made this procedure impossible until I was clear of the drug for several days. Otherwise I could bleed out, but it could also be dangerous to be off the blood thinner for fear of stroke from the atrial fib. I would have to stay in ICU until the catheterization had been completed.

Meanwhile, my family and close friends and colleagues from various parts of the country wanted to be with me in Omaha. Not a good idea. Ed and my sister Joan decided that only one needed to be there. My older sister won the toss, arriving the day I had the catheterization. The procedure, not an operation, was painless, but upon completion I had to lie absolutely flat for five or six hours with heavy sandbags on my groin. Bleeding was a problem from this procedure even if blood thinners were not in my system.

I was so relieved to see my sister. David picked her up at the airport, drove her to the hospital, found and delivered her to a nearby hotel and even took us to the airport when we left Omaha five days later. He and the others from their brokerage office were part of a steady stream of visitors, along with John Kappert, manager of the company in Nebraska.

When the report from the catheterization came in, it was revealed that I had one artery blocked about fifty percent, but I was told that sometimes blockage temporarily disappears right after a heart attack. There was heart damage, but they couldn't tell how much. It appeared that the blockage showed up in the left anterior descending artery, sometimes referred to as "the widow maker."

My sister could take me home on Sunday. She and David arranged everything for my Omaha departure. I was weak, tired and my groin and chest hurt. The hospital gave me a DVD of the cardiac catheterization, dialogue from doctors and test findings for me to give to my cardiologist, Dr. Patricia Caldwell, at The Ohio State University Hospital.

The flight back to Columbus with a change of planes in St. Louis was difficult even with the wheelchair that my sister had ordered. My carefree attitude and confidence had changed in less than a week. I had been working for Bob Harris and his sons Peter and Jim for twenty-three years, traveling all over the country almost every week Tuesday to Friday. I loved my job.

Three years before, Ed and I had met and fell in love. We talked about marriage, but marriage wasn't necessary for us to be happy together. He ran his own company and traveled a lot, but not as much as I did. We had a lot in common and enjoyed going out to sporting events, plays, concerts, good restaurants and playing golf. We went on vacations together. In February, just a month before my heart attack, we had been to Australia on an all-expenses paid trip for Ed to make a couple of speeches. As Ed's significant other I went with all expenses paid too.

Now I was damaged. Would I be able to do what I had been doing professionally, socially and emotionally? Would Ed want out of this relationship, or would he feel sorry for me? Either way, life had changed but I wasn't giving in or giving up.

CHAPTER TWO
1980

Twenty years before the Omaha heart attack I recalled my first unrelated heart episode. I chose to ignore it. I was not yet forty-three. Infallible.

§

Sheila, the ninety-year-old aerobics instructor, was yelling over the music set to a rhythm that made the thirty women in the gym at the Louisville Jewish Community Center dance and sweat: "Right leg lunge front, lunge back, side step right, side step left and side step right. Repeat other leg. Run in place count ten."

We had been going at it like this for almost an hour. Now

it was time for a cool down and a drink of water. "OK, girls; let's walk clockwise at a brisk pace around the room, then leisurely twice around the room while you take your pulse. Then we'll stretch."

Rita, my Louisville friend for many years, always invited me to stay with her whenever I worked in the Kentucky area. Days on the road started early but ended around four in the afternoon. Working Kentucky markets three or four times a year gave me the opportunity to see my friend and save money for my company by staying at her home instead of a hotel.

She and I usually tried to get into one of Sheila's aerobic classes, which wasn't easy. Everyone in Louisville loved the workout from the trim muscled woman who, at ninety, was in better shape than women half her age. "Slow down your pace and check your pulse," she yelled out over music.

I couldn't find my pulse. I stopped walking to check it further. Here it is, or is it? I felt movement inside my right wrist using the index finger from my left hand, but I couldn't get a count. First it was fast: boom, boom, boom, then faster like a hovering hummingbird's wings. Finally it slowed down but not enough to count the beats. Oops, there it goes again. Regular beats for a few seconds then it stopped altogether for a second, maybe two. Now the hummingbird wings again. What is this? Well, I did the workout and I feel just fine. I'm not going to worry about it, I said to myself. And, I didn't. That night and the next day I took my pulse as I had after the workout and the beats were steady and normal. Maybe the unsteady rhythm was a fluke. I forgot about it.

That was my first experience of what I know now as atrial fibrillation. If I went into the weird heartbeat, I couldn't feel it. So, if I couldn't feel it, it didn't exist...in my mind. At forty-three, I'd never even heard the term atrial fibrillation.

Growing up, my parents and their friends would discuss people they knew who had heart trouble, a term then used for any abnormality in the upper chest. Some of them had massive heart attacks or strokes. My mother was afraid of strokes because the people who got them were often partially paralyzed and sometimes couldn't talk. Could they think? Wouldn't it be awful to know you were paralyzed and deformed physically from a stroke, unable to speak, but your mind worked fully and no one knew it? My mother didn't want to depend on someone taking care of her. Losing her independence was the worst thing she could think of. As it was, when she did have a heart attack, she asked my sister and me if she had had a stroke. We told her that she had not. She seemed relieved, but she only lived twelve hours more. That was 1978. If it had been today, with all the progress made in managing heart complications, her life may have been different.

It didn't occur to me that both parents as well as an older sister, aunts, cousins and uncles suffered from heart issues. It was known then that genetics played the biggest part for developing all heart disease, but I also knew about problems caused by foods we eat.

Cholesterol was a word gaining popularity for clogging arteries and limiting blood flow to the heart. I had just started my career in the food industry and the products I sold were reduced fat margarine and processed cheese under the Weight Watchers label. We advertised that our margarine was the healthiest with a three to one ratio of polyunsaturated to saturated fat, a healthy ratio to reduce or keep bad cholesterol in check. It was on the shelves at all grocery stores. My parents would proudly check and straighten shelf stock of my products each time they went shopping.

So, when my mother's heart attack became fatal, I began to place more importance on my own medical issues. Furthermore, a few years later when my father's heart attack allowed him to linger a little longer than Mother, I realized that my heritage and preservation depended on me.

§

The 1980 Louisville bout with atrial fib was not my first incidence of health problems. A string of incurable but manageable diseases and viruses invaded my body starting when I was fifteen, in the 1950s. I came down with glandular fever, or mononucleosis, as it was sometimes called, which carried with it hepatitis. Neither my family nor I had ever heard of any of the three. As hepatitis affects the liver, I was required to spend a few days in the hospital, and was then sent home to rest for weeks while trying to keep up with high school work. The worst part of this illness was being so tired even when it was supposedly over and I was allowed to go back to school. The lingering effects are still in my blood and recognizable by health care workers who must be warned to wear plastic gloves while caring for me. I can never donate blood or any of my organs upon my death. Another possible difficulty with hepatitis is that it can do harm to the liver and I must be cautious of how much alcohol I consume and limit fried foods, both of which are fairly easy for me to do. Hepatitis has reared its ugly head on the few occasions that I've needed surgery. In case I need to be given blood during these procedures, it is suggested that I prepare ahead of time by giving and storing my own blood before the surgical events take place.

In the early 1960s, after the births of my two children, Mark and Brian, another chronic problem began while we were living in Los Angeles, California. As a young mother I thought that feeling tired all of the time, even when I woke up in the morning, was normal. Then I started gaining weight as my whole body became listless. My hair thinned and went limp. My nails peeled like layers of tissue paper. My skin became dry and flakey. The family doctor gave me thyroid pills that helped a little with the fatigue but not the weight gain. Finally, he prescribed "diet pills." These amphetamines were time released green capsules that kept me alert, full of energy and not hungry all day long. I loved them and figured that the thyroid and diet pills worked hand in hand to cure me. When the thirty-day supply of green gremlins ran out, the doctor's office called the pharmacist for another supply. Eventually the prescription came with four or five automatic refills.

Everyone was taking diet pills to lose weight. After a couple of months they didn't work so well, but I was addicted. If I took two, I could get the same effect: energy galore, sporadic appetite, alert behavior. This went on for a couple of years while I worked as a copywriter for a television station and then began a career in the Los Angeles fashion industry. I wasn't naïve about addictions. The rhetoric surrounding diet pills was everywhere, especially since a new book and then the movie, *Valley of The Dolls,* came out and made stars of a young cast portraying women addicted to all kinds of pills.

Being thin was a good thing that came with guilt. I knew that I had to get off the diet pills and find an endocrinologist as I was sure I had a thyroid problem. The diet pills weren't so easy to get anymore. My friend Esther, a petite size four, decided to go off cold turkey. I didn't see her for many months. By the time we met for lunch in an outdoor Hollywood restaurant, I didn't recognize her. She had blown up more than twice her size, and she ate everything she could get onto a fork, from her plate and mine. She even ordered dessert, something no one does publicly if you work in the industry in Los Angeles.

"Get off the pills," she said. "They'll own you if you don't, but do it sensibly. If you can do it gradually, that's the best way." She looked down at her chubby hands and went on, "I didn't do that. I didn't have enough of a supply. I was afraid. Look at me. I'm a fat mess."

I found an endocrinologist in the Wilshire District of LA, and the journey began. Starting with one prescribed diet pill daily the first week, the gradual process of one every other day and then one every three days until almost a month later I was free. I felt awful. The thyroid medication wasn't working. The doctor changed it, and then he increased the dosage. I started shaking. He lowered the amount. I was tired and draggy. My weight went up. It took a long time for my system to absorb, stabilize and adjust. Just as it did, my doctor made a frightening discovery during a routine examination. He sent me to the lab for tests. I had tumors on my thyroid gland. Then he recommended a surgeon. I was thirty years old with tumors that could be thyroid cancer.

During one of the appointments with endocrinology surgeon Dr. Daniel Fortmann, he asked me if I was from Ohio. Pretty amazing for a doctor in Los Angeles who had probably never been to Ohio. "Yes," I said. "How'd you know?"

"I see a lot of Ohio patients with thyroid problems." I looked at him questionably while he examined my throat area and explained, "During the Ice Age a long time ago, Ohio was covered with sheets of ice. When it melted, the water in rivers, streams, soil and rock was void of iodine, leaving food and water supplies without enough iodine to produce the hormones needed for thyroid glands."

Was that why my mother stressed using Morton Iodized Salt for flavor and cooking? The tubular blue container came with the written claim on its label: *This salt supplies iodide, a necessary nutrient.*

Dr. Fortmann had good credentials as a surgeon. And, he'd had another career. In 1965 he had been admitted to the Football Hall of Fame for his success as offensive guard while playing for the Chicago Bears. He played for the Bears while he went to medical school in Chicago. My personal hall of fame honored him when he announced, after surgery, that the tumors were benign but that he had had to remove almost all of my thyroid gland. He showed me how he had made the incision in the fold of my neck revealing hardly any scar. Then he suggested that the man in my life buy a diamond necklace to cover leftover scar evidence.

The medications managed my thyroid problems, more or less, for over ten years. Sometimes the drug companies would change or discontinue making the drug that helped me most, and my body reacted in ways I recognized as thyroid deficient. When the correct or new meds were found, after a few weeks I would feel better.

In the late 1970s I moved back to my home in Ohio from California. With some difficulty I found Dr. Sam Cataland, endocrinologist at The Ohio State University Medical Center in Columbus. During a scheduled appointment a few years later while he was listening to my heart, he stopped and asked how I was feeling. I said, "Sleepy and not good, but I can't really describe it." He listened to my heart again and then took my pulse in different places, wrists and neck.

"You are in atrial fibrillation. Are you aware of that?"

"What exactly is that?" I asked.

"It's an irregular heartbeat but it's more than that. It can be dangerous." Again he started the examination by listening to my heart, front and back and neck. Then he tried to count the beats. Having a difficult time finding the pulse and counting, he folded his stethoscope and put it back in his pocket. "Have you ever felt this way before or been told you have atrial fibrillation?"

I told him about the other time I couldn't get a regular pulse, and that once my gynecologist told me that I had an irregular heartbeat. "But, Dr. Cataland, I didn't feel badly so I just ignored it. I still exercise several times a week even when I don't feel great. I just figured it to be my thyroid."

Dr. Cataland looked worried as he said, "I'm going to call Dr. Patricia Caldwell, a cardiologist upstairs in this building. I want you to see her as soon as possible. Don't put this off."

CHAPTER THREE
1982

In 1982 at age forty-five, I was considered young. Maybe early middle age, but not yet at a time for chronic problems deemed for the elderly. Dr. Patricia Caldwell became my cardiologist at The Ohio State University Medical Center then and for the next twenty years, a generation. She guided and protected me through two ten-year phases of atrial fibrillation but without the benefit or the knowledge and technology available to today's electrophysiologists. Atrial fibrillation is an electrical problem in the upper chambers of the heart.

The OSU Medical Center is a teaching hospital. Medical students, interns and residents follow doctors on their rounds and clinic appointments as part of their training. Some patients don't like the audience of a learning staff, but I welcomed the assistants and they taught me valuable lessons. Among them to pay attention, to listen and to ask my own questions, probing for answers when I didn't understand.

By the mid-1980s, I was aware of atrial fibrillation and what it did and did not do to my body. Initially, tests to make sure mine was atrial and not a ventricular problem gave me relief. I was informed that atrial was not as serious as ventricular. They are different problems. I wasn't in atrial fib all the time, not even most of the time. Sometimes I had to feel my pulse to find out, other times it grabbed hold of me like an earthquake.

I trusted Dr. Caldwell. But, I tried to get around her suggestions. I'm in sales and have been told that I'm pretty good at it. For several years I sold her on the idea that I didn't need to take the blood thinner warfarin. Relatively young, just under fifty and single, I didn't want my social life marred with purplish/red blotches if I bumped an arm or a leg or if the bruises appeared mysteriously without provocation.

Dr. Caldwell was somewhat younger than I, serious but good-humored and well organized with a good memory. Her office was in the old Clinic Building on an upper floor between two examining rooms. After seeing a patient she went into the middle office and dictated her notes and findings into a tape recorder. Sitting in one of the neighboring exam rooms, I could

28

hear every word she spoke and was way ahead of her when she came back in for consultation before the blood draw or final instructions. My appointments were every few months unless I had a problem or was forced to wear a heart monitor for a period of time.

When I first started seeing Dr. Caldwell, her black page-boy haircut had flecks of gray. She was shorter than I, well-built and pleasant. Later, at retirement age, she looked the same, but her hair was almost all gray. Initially, after tests and explanations about the nature and history of atrial fibrillation, she asked me to keep a diary and to document whenever I felt any irregularity in my pulse. By now, I was feeling the A-Fib when it happened, but I still ignored it until the irregularity went from a few minutes of constant fluttering and skipping beats to several hours. I was getting scared. Was the anxiety I felt from the rapid heartbeat or emotional upheaval? Either way, I had a tough time breathing.

Was it caused by something I ate or didn't eat or too much exercise or not enough? It didn't seem that way. I was instruct-ed not to drink or eat anything with caffeine or alcohol, but still the A-Fib came. I started tracking the episodes. For a while I would go into the chaotic heartbeat every ten days and it last-ed from two hours to twelve or fourteen. Dr. Caldwell said to telephone her if I was in A-Fib for eighteen hours or longer. I was. Sometimes I woke up with it, other times it came when I was doing nothing. I tried to relate it to stress, to steak, to too much sleep or not enough sleep. There was no pattern. I tested it. I had some wine and nothing happened. The next time I had wine, I went into atrial fib.

"Are you in or out, Mrs. Linver?" She always referred to me that way, never as Rosalie.

"You know, Dr. Caldwell, I get confused whether 'in' means in atrial fib or 'in' regular rhythm." She explained what she meant, but I never got it. I still use being in A-Fib as "in."

Atrial fib was coming more often and with more intensity. I could almost always feel it now. It was interfering with my life and my job. As regional sales manager, I was the only salesperson. For several years, I managed food brokers all over the country. We sold Weight Watchers Margarine and Cheese and a variety of foods under that label. I was on the road every week Tuesday through Thursday or Friday flying to major cities or driving if the destination was within 200 miles.

Each episode exhausted me more and more. "I can't protect you unless you take a blood thinner," Dr. Caldwell said. She was in an explosive mood and I was being flip. We were in an examining room. She listened to my heart then put the stethoscope on the table. I was in A-Fib. "It's unlikely you'll die from A-Fib, but you can have a stroke. You need to be on warfarin."

"Is that the same as Coumadin?" I asked.

"Coumadin is the brand. Warfarin is the generic name."

"I'm taking the Digoxin you prescribed, but it seems that I'm in A-Fib more now than ever. What does Digoxin do that warfarin doesn't?"

"When you're in A-Fib, sometimes the heart rate can go as dangerously high as two hundred beats per minute. Digoxin slows your heart."

What she didn't tell me then is that the Digoxin slows the heart rate all of the time. So, yes, I was protected if it was lowered from 200 beats per minute. It also reduced the beats per minute when I was not in A-Fib. A regular rhythm of seventy beats could slow to forty or less with Digoxin in the system. That is what happened to me.

Dr. Caldwell insisted I go on the blood thinner warfarin. "When you're in A-Fib, the blood isn't moving smoothly. It can pool in the atrium and cause a stroke. The warfarin will protect you by keeping the blood moving."

"Are there side effects? Will I have restrictions? How's it regulated? Will it interfere with my lifestyle?"

"It's hard to regulate at times and necessary for you to have regular INR tests to check blood levels."

"What's INR?" I asked.

"It stands for International Normalized Ratio, which is the

test for blood clotting levels. You'll need to be tested every two or three weeks. There are several labs for you to choose from. You can come to this building downstairs on the first floor, or OSU Hospital East on Broad Street." She named a couple other locations and was sure to insert a positive by telling me that I didn't need an appointment.

Having a blood test every two or three weeks gave me a new set of friends. Soon I learned which technicians on the blood-taking staff did a good job of extracting blood and who had trouble finding the veins. Cleo was my favorite.

That day or the day after, I would get a call from the lab telling me if my INR was satisfactory or not. If too high, I was instructed to take less warfarin so I wouldn't bleed internally. If too low, the dose was increased slightly. Leafy green vegetables could lower levels if I ate them sporadically. Aspirin was a no-no in almost all cases. If a new medication, either prescription or over-the-counter, was introduced, levels had to be checked right away. It was dangerous for me to be around sharp objects, as a cut or injury could result in too much bleeding. I was advised not to shave my legs.

Cases of atrial fibrillation were becoming more commonly diagnosed. New drugs to regulate it were entering the market all the time. Dr. Caldwell had me try several. None worked. Some gave me flu symptoms or joint pain or threw me into atrial fib more severely. Occasionally, when a new one came along she suggested I try it as an in-patient for three days. If the drug didn't work, it would be evident within the first seventy-two hours, and if I were under surveillance and monitored, I would be safe from harmful effects. Over the years, I did four drug in-patient trials. One worked while I was in the hospital and stopped as soon as I got home. The others didn't work at all.

I read in *Time* magazine that a new procedure called a cardiac ablation was being tested at University of Michigan. I asked Dr. Caldwell about it. "Right now, Mrs. Linver, it's too new and not enough is known about the ablation. We'll have to watch and wait. We're enlarging our Electrophysiology Department to do more research on arrhythmias." Electrophysiology was a new word in my vocabulary, and I would hear it often.

In 1990 I flew to Adelaide, Australia, a twenty-hour trip from Columbus with stops in St. Louis, Los Angeles and Auckland, New Zealand. An eight hour delay in Auckland made the trip almost thirty hours long. As we pulled out of Columbus I felt the now familiar beginnings of atrial fib which lasted all the way to my destination. Coupled with jet lag, the visit with my friend Krystyna got off to a very precarious start, especially since I didn't share my medical problems with her.

CHAPTER FOUR
1986

Self-pity was not my bailiwick. Sure, I became depressed from time to time, but it didn't last long. Depression uses too much energy, and I like to feel good. Usually I could work my way out of it, first by wallowing in a pity party for a day or a few hours, then doing something nice for myself besides eating—going to a movie, reading a book or finally realizing how good I had it and how my mother would react.

Mother wasn't tolerant of people's self-absorption or constant complaining. When I was young, if I didn't feel well enough to go to school, she insisted I go unless I had a fever. She never believed in depression or self-pity or debilitating illnesses, telling me that "such-n-such" walked around taking her pulse all the time to see if she was sick or having a heart attack. Consequently, I've always just figured that aches and pains were part of life and that the body is like a car that needs periodic checkups, repairs and sometimes replacement parts.

So, when Dr. Caldwell told me to check my pulse once or twice a day to see if I was in atrial fib, I remembered my mother's words and tried surreptitiously to hold my index finger on the inside, while the thumb was on the opposite side of the wrist. I counted the heartbeats and hoped the rhythm was smooth. When not in the weird heartbeat, I could count forty steady beats per minute. When I was in atrial fib, there was a flutter, then five or six or twenty slow beats, then some too fast to count. Now I noticed something new: an occasional pause between beats for a couple or more seconds. When did that start? Ignoring the pauses, I reminded myself to tell Dr. Caldwell at my next appointment.

I couldn't make plans. I never knew how I was going to feel. If I planned a tennis date or a hike or an out of town weekend or vacation and I had an episode of atrial fib, the effort and fear wasn't worth it. I tried to stick to plays and concerts and activities that didn't require physical effort and stamina. When I wasn't in atrial fib I could do anything, but I never knew when the now-familiar shortness of breath was going to invade my chest. I chose not to share my complaints with anyone except Dr. Caldwell.

She suggested I try the anti-arrhythmia drug amiodarone, a potentially dangerous drug. An in-patient drug trial proved to be successful. I was on that drug for nineteen years. It worked ninety percent of the time. The other ten percent was no better or worse than it had been without amiodarone. Fortunately, the drug's serious side effects left me alone. The not-so serious effects were burdensome and sometimes hard to manage.

Without knowing I was depressed, I kept up with work and my friends, family and social life at home and on the job. But I stopped all exercise and my eating was out of control. I had joined Weight Watchers several times in the past and knew how and what to eat and what I should weigh. Besides that, I was Regional Sales Manager for the company that manufactured some Weight Watchers products. I trained sales people how to be effective at selling our items, but I wasn't paying attention to what I knew was right for me.

I couldn't stand the way I looked or the way I felt. My clothes didn't fit and I was out of breath going up a flight of steps, even when I wasn't in atrial fib. I was so out of shape. I saw a photograph of myself and hated it. Now at age forty-nine I looked dreary and matronly and thick. Preparing to enter fifty looking and feeling like I did was inexcusable. I was embarrassed even to think that I had been the head of a fashion college in Los Angeles.

I spoke to my fat face in the mirror. The conversation was straightforward and stern. Forcing myself to look closely at the extra chin and roll of fat in my middle, I turned sideways and stared at rounded shoulders and disgusting posture. "Who are you?" I screamed. I had to take back my life!

§

In 1986 a supermarket chain in Pittsburgh began a summer promotion by introducing customers to fruits and vegetables that were healthy and interesting and in some cases unfamiliar. They tied it to special sales, coupons and an exercise program that promoted walking. They offered Buy One Get One Free opportunities such as "buy a quart of fresh strawberries and get a low-fat or fat-free topping free." A nutritionist and personal trainer were stationed in the produce section at specific times to offer advice and answer questions. Recipes were offered and customers competed with their own for prizes. It was a great idea for the supermarkets and their customers. Grocers all over the country got on the wagon with Produce + Walking = Good Health.

I sold some of the food chains on displaying and selling our low-fat margarine and cheese in the produce section too. The specialists involved organized walks around the outside parking lots. Soon beverage sales and even athletic equipment, including shoes, were available for new walkers to buy at the walkathons.

Though I was familiar with all the produce, the promotion pushed me into the walking. The trainers suggested that customers start with an easy fifteen-minute walk every day at a brisk pace but not an uncomfortable one. After a week the walk should go to an easy thirty minutes. I started doing this because it was summer and I could walk wherever I was working—Detroit, St. Louis, Chicago or at home. The hotels where I stayed when I was working in various cities were in safe neighborhoods. I could walk outside early in the morning or after work before dinner. Sometimes I would drive to a park area where there were walking paths around a lake or grounds. It stayed light outside until eight or nine o'clock and was usually light by six in the morning.

After the second week, supermarket trainers suggested we pick up the pace on our walks and time ourselves as to how far we could walk in fifteen or thirty minutes. Some walking paths had mile markers and I could do a mile in twenty minutes. They also suggested investing in a good pair of walking shoes. I did. After a month, the final leg of the promotion was presented: "Walk forty-five minutes every day or at least five days per week." They proclaimed that along with a diet high in fruits and vegetables, we would be fit for life. Artichokes were introduced as vegetable-of-the-week along with recipes and demonstrations showing customers how to prepare the thistle-like herb with an edible flower head. Because melted butter or mayonnaise is often used for dipping artichoke parts, I was granted permission from my company to offer grocery stores coupons good for Weight Watchers Margarine and Mayonnaise.

When I started walking, a beautiful part of my life began. Walking was more than exercise. It was like brushing my teeth: I had to do it to feel good. Atrial fib was still in my life, but somehow I had to walk even when I was in atrial fib. I told Dr. Caldwell about it.

"Do you walk fast when you're in A-Fib?" she asked.

"Yes," I said, "but now I carry a card with my personal information in case I pass out on the path."

Her only reply was, "Usually one doesn't die from atrial fib. The danger is a stroke."

"But, with the warfarin to keep blood moving and amiodarone for arrhythmia, do you think I'll be OK?"

She looked at me, lifted the stethoscope to my chest and told me to take a deep breath.

When the days became shorter and there was less light and the weather got colder and more unpredictable, I still walked outside. Bundling my body in a flannel-lined jogging suit over long silk underwear, scarf, gloves and a knitted cap, I embraced the frosty fresh air. Rosy cheeks and itchy skin exposed in the cold made me smile and feel alive.

I discovered that most of the hotels on the road had workout facilities and usually a treadmill or two or three. I watched as other guests used the walking machine and I copied them, reluctantly at first, then cautiously I got the hang of it. A television set within my vision made the time go faster, but I was afraid it would disturb my concentration and I could fall, so I kept the TV off.

By now I was walking an hour, going more than three miles. Soon it became four miles in an hour, and since the treadmills calculated calories used during the walk, I saw that I was using almost one hundred calories per mile, practically 400 calories that hour.

I couldn't walk four fifteen-minute miles every day. It was too much for my body. My legs and lower back were sore, but I did buy a treadmill for my home. Between the hotel and my home treadmill, I was walking four or five days a week. I wasn't eating as much as before, but still I made bad selections at the restaurants on the road. Much of the overeating was from boredom. After working all day away from home and friends, I sometimes went to the mall or to a movie or to dinner with people I worked with. Most of my co-workers were men, but if we had dinner together, they often invited their families or invited me into their homes. In the eighties and early nineties few salespeople carried laptop computers, so working in the hotel room at night wasn't yet part of the job.

Food was my only problem, besides the regular bouts of atrial fib. I decided to enroll again in the Weight Watchers program. This would be my fourth time in twenty years, always losing most of the weight but never completing the program to stay at my own goal long enough to receive the certificate. I've lost 800 pounds during my lifetime, the same twenty pounds forty times. I've been on every diet out there, even taking a daily shot of something from the placenta of pregnant women, eating 500 calories and drinking twelve glasses of water daily.

With their award, I could go to a Weight Watchers meeting anywhere anytime without paying the dues as long as I was within two pounds of goal at weigh-in. A mental stabilizer for behavior modification with food, the weekly meetings were a crutch that I needed at that time. The weigh-ins before each meeting were held in private. The reward earned for the hard work of keeping a food diary, making good eating choices and paying attention to everything that went into the mouth was a weight loss. Even a fraction of a pound meant success.

Sometimes while standing in front of the kitchen sink, I ate something I knew I didn't really want and shouldn't have.

Just before swallowing the forbidden food, I spit it out before my body became a human garbage can. I learned other food tricks: putting the fork down between bites slows eating; the mind doesn't know that the stomach is full for at least twenty minutes. Being full doesn't always make one stop eating. Another trick I still use is to put meals on smaller plates and in smaller bowls. It looks like more food.

I became obsessed with cooking food that was legal on the Weight Watchers program. Volume was as important as taste. Vegetables allowed me to eat all day long. I spent weekends cooking, making vegetable soups, pasta from spaghetti squash, pancakes from pineapple and dry non-fat milk, mashed cauliflower that tasted like potatoes, roasted skinless chicken breasts with vegetables and soy sauce. After I devoured the chicken, I gnawed and sucked on the bones. The little pile of bones looked like chopped toothpicks.

I invented a snack made from the peel of an orange, one of three fruit servings allowed daily. Cutting the peel into squares less than an inch long, sprinkling them with sugar substitute, cinnamon and nutmeg, I put them under the broiler for a minute. Cooled, the squares were crisp and chewy, though bitter.

The vegetable soup was a staple item that I always kept on hand. It became thicker and tastier the older it got. I renamed it vegetable compote. My sixteen quart pot of soup simmered stove top all day long. It was so big I couldn't see over the top. I didn't have a spoon long enough to stir it, losing spoons that reappeared when I emptied the mixture into smaller containers. The pot was so heavy I couldn't lift it. But, vegetable compote was always available in my refrigerator or freezer. It never let me down.

VEGETABLE COMPOTE

One or two 48 ounce cans of tomato juice or V-8 Juice (or one can of each)

Equal amounts of water

Two or three quarts of fat-free chicken broth

Large head of shredded cabbage

Six to eight large, deep-orange carrots peeled and sliced into half-inch thick quarters

Two large sliced onions

Two or three cups of celery, chopped

Cut up turnips and/or parsnips

Bring above items to boil. Then throw in every vegetable from your cupboard, refrigerator and freezer. Add any and every spice you like.

Variations to the bloat boat servings of vegetable compote: slice a kosher hot dog in it to make a complete meal of vegetables and protein. Or, put some of the cold mixture (without hot dogs) into a blender to puree and drink as a refreshing cold soup or gazpacho.

Another method to combat bad food choices: Before going to a party, I eat a little something so as not to be starving when I arrive. Hunger results in eating empty calories. A single serving of dry Cheerios or bite size Shredded Wheat right out of the box and a glass of water takes the edge off.

The weight came off. The Weight Watchers certificate was ceremoniously presented to me four weeks before my fiftieth birthday in 1987. I was in control of my body once more, and it went on that way for ten more years, the atrial fib getting slightly worse every year. I was used to it and lived in the moment not knowing that I would then go through five surgeries in a three-year period.

CHAPTER FIVE
1997-1998

My company sold the Weight Watchers items to a major conglomerate in the late 1980s. We still owned other food items, not under that label. I was offered a position to stay with the company, managing the leftover labels, and helping to start a new line of heart-healthy foods. Two of us in sales were managing food brokers throughout the entire country. I was still flying somewhere from Columbus every week in the days when flying was still fun, accumulating airline frequent flyer points by the thousands.

Atrial fib still occurred when I least expected and wasn't prepared to deal with it. Dr. Caldwell had me wear heart monitors as new devices came on the market. For a month I carried one in my purse. It looked like a garage door opener. When I felt the beginnings of A-Fib, I called a number in Columbus from whatever city I was in and held the device over my heart and the telephone receiver over it…or something like that. I often wondered how many garage doors went up or closed in the neighborhood.

Exercise was my salvation. I was addicted to walking every day that I wasn't in atrial fib. Now I played tennis too. If I flew home on a Thursday or Friday by 5:30, I'd go directly to the hospital blood draw to get the INR, or keep my appointment with Dr. Caldwell. Most of the time I felt in control of my body actions and it was a good life.

My children were happily married, and I became a grandmother three times. On my sixtieth birthday I met and fell in love with Ed. We had a wonderful courtship. When I discovered his love for golf, a game I had watched occasionally but had never played, I realized that if this relationship was going anywhere, I had better learn to play. I took three lessons a week and hit balls at a golf range some evenings. The game took a lot of time and patience for both Ed and me.

Golf is the most difficult physical endeavor I have ever attempted. Hitting a stationary ball is unnatural, especially while keeping the head absolutely still, looking at where the ball was, not where it is going. Besides skill, the game of golf takes a clear head, plenty of stamina and a minimum of four hours of energy to complete eighteen holes, each one a mini game in itself. The real test is to not let the mistakes of the last hole played influence the next one. It's crazy fun, but not when in A-Fib.

Our first vacation together was between Christmas and New Year's at a hotel on the beach in Florida. We played tennis, went for long walks in the sand, played golf and got to know each other. Then I started having a problem walking, especially up and down steps or in and out of a car. I figured I pulled a muscle in my groin. The pain was mild at first but continued after we returned home and I started back to work.

I made an appointment with an orthopedic doctor. "I think I pulled my right groin muscle."

"Let's take an x-ray and see," he said. When he joined me back in the examining room, he posted the x-ray on a lighted wall screen and pointed to what I thought was my groin, but it wasn't. "Your problem is your hip, not your groin."

"I thought the hip was around toward the back and a little higher," I said.

"This ball joint is your hip," he said, pointing to the top of my leg where it connects to the hip with a rotating ball. "Right now arthritis has taken over and you practically have no cartilage left to cushion the movement when you walk and move that joint connection. Eventually you will lose all of the carti-lage and the joint between leg and hip will be bone-on-bone."

"What is eventually? Next week? Next year? Then, what?" I asked.

"You'll need a hip replacement. Meanwhile, I'll give you prescriptions for pain and an anti-inflammatory. You could go six months or a year depending on your pain tolerance. Bone-on-bone hurts."

He seemed so casual about this shocking information. I knew nothing about arthritis except that my mother had had it in her legs. Maybe it was her hips. I remembered that when I went with her to the grocery store, she always insisted that she, not I, push the grocery cart for something to hold onto as we shopped for food. She limped a little, but never complained. Mother never had a hip replacement. Maybe there was no such thing in the 1970s, but if she felt the pain I was feeling, she had it for the rest of her life. I had a pretty high pain tolerance, but Mother's must have been incredible.

My cousin Jerry who owned the pharmacy where I bought all my medications had problems with his knees. He had both knees replaced just a couple of years before. He educated me in full about who to see, what to do and when to do it.

"But how can I have surgery with my atrial fib?" I asked. "What about the blood thinner?"

"There are ways," Jerry said. "First you have to see other orthopedic surgeons and get more opinions."

"Who replaced your knees?" I asked.

Jerry recommended that I make an appointment with his orthopedic surgeon, Dr. David Halley, who only operated on knees and hips. His office waiting room was full when I arrived, but only half the people there were patients. Spouses, family or caregivers made up the other half because patients weren't permitted to drive for a period of time after surgery. All the chairs in the waiting room were straight back with seats higher than normal. During recovery from hip and knee surgeries the hips must always be higher than the knees, never lower. Lower puts too much pressure on the joints when sitting down or getting up. A variety of canes, crutches and walkers belonged to the waiting patients. The steady stream of elderly men and women went from x-ray to examining room to consulting, and then to a window where follow-up appointments were made.

The doctor's staff seemed efficient, plentiful and well organized. The patient rooms were never empty. While one patient was getting an x-ray, another was being examined while another was consulting with Dr. Halley or scheduling surgery. I was part of an assembly line, but I didn't have to wait long. I liked Dr. Halley right away. He was a big man about my age and he walked with a mild limp. Possibly he was in need of knee surgery. He was jovial, not loud, but he could be heard going in and out of examining rooms either spewing his verbal notes into a recorder or giving comfort and instructions to patients.

"So you're Jerry's cousin! He called me about you," Dr. Halley said as we looked at the x-rays of both hips, not just the one that hurt. "Your right hip has almost no cartilage now," he said, pointing to the naked ball joint. "Your left hip is not in great condition either. It will need to be replaced probably within a year after the right hip." He was authoritative and sure of himself.

"I've read that hip replacements only last for ten or fifteen years," I said. "I'm only sixty. Would I need to have hip replacements more than once?"

"Not necessarily. It depends on the materials used and what new parts are available at the time. It also depends on your physical condition and recovery. Replacements have become so common and proficient that someday they'll be done drive-thru."

I loved his sense of humor and his use of the phrase, "what new parts are available."

"I've also heard that I should wait until I can't stand the pain anymore before having the surgery. Do you agree?"

"It's up to you, but you can schedule the surgery on the

right hip anytime you want." His hands were crossed and resting in his lap. "However," he said, lifting two fingers and pointing them at me, "when it becomes too difficult to walk, your gait will change because of the pain. If you wait too long, your gait may not go back to normal after the surgery. Also, your left hip will get worse as you can see from the x-rays, and it will be difficult for you to walk at all with cartilage gone in both hips."

Then I told him about my atrial fib and the medications I took. I also told him that I had had hepatitis as a teenager. Tainted blood. How would that affect hip surgery? He had reasonable answers for all my worrisome questions and made me feel safe and secure about moving ahead.

"I travel in my job, Dr. Halley. How long will I have to recover?"

"Recovery is eight weeks under normal conditions," he said. "During that time you won't be able to drive, cross your legs, sit on a regular toilet seat or soft furniture that you would sink into. You won't be permitted to bend or stoop or step into a bathtub. My approach to rehabilitation is only walking, but plenty of it. You will carry a square hard foam pillow to sit on everywhere you go including in the car, restaurants and home. That is so that your hips will be higher than your knees during recovery." He got up, gathering the x-rays and put his hand on my shoulder guiding me toward the door.

"You'll be instructed how to use equipment like a fetcher to pick up things. You'll have a gadget to help you slip on shoes and put on socks without bending. You can use soap on a rope so it doesn't fall in the shower as long as it's a walk-in shower. Home care will show you how to do all of this. Do you have someone to help you after surgery?"

"I don't know yet," I said. I was still thinking about the eight weeks of not driving. My boss, Bob, in New Jersey was not going to be happy. He wasn't good in handling time off, though I could certainly work from home and do just as much selling and managing my group of food brokers by telephone and email. After twenty years of employment with his company, Bob complained whenever I took any of my two weeks annual vacation.

"My condo is two-story. What about going up and down stairs?"

"You can go up and down once a day for the first two or three weeks, slowly and one step at a time." Dr. Halley gave me more prescriptions for pain and another anti-inflammatory and told me to call him when I had trouble sleeping because turning over in bed would become too painful. That's when I would know it was time to get that hip replaced.

I called my boss with the news. He said he didn't know I was having hip problems, but we rarely saw each other unless we had a sales meeting at his office in New Jersey or he joined me for one of my trips to a market in the South or Midwest. I consulted him about when the best time would be for me to have the surgery. I suggested early June. Currently it was April.

"How long will you be recovering?" Bob asked.

"Dr. Halley says I can't drive for eight weeks. During the first two weeks I will need help. My sister Joan has offered to take care of me at her house. After that I'll go home and work there until I can travel again."

"Eight weeks," he said in a voice louder than normal. "I can't let you take eight weeks off."

"Well, Bob, I'd be happy to let you talk to Dr. Halley," I said. I knew he'd react this way. "After the first two weeks, I'll be able to work from home, make sales calls by phone and email and even have local meetings at my house. Besides, I'll work with our Columbus broker and have their people shuffle me around to stores and sales offices."

"I can't run a business with only Scott on the West Coast," he said.

I was getting angry. "It seems to me, Bob, that if I'm that important to this company, you aren't paying me enough."

"We'll talk later. I have to take another call," he said conveniently, though I didn't hear Kathy's voice on the intercom telling him that he had another call.

This was not the first time we'd had fighting words about employment issues. I knew there could be blasts of temper from both of us. I was usually careful about answering back, especially since both sons had left the business over the last few years. I loved working for his boys, but Peter left to start his own business, also in the food industry, and Jim decided to go to law school. Now it was just Scott in California and me in Ohio. We were covering the country.

The pain got worse and I hated taking pain pills. I couldn't focus and every step was agony. Cartilage in the right hip was long gone. Sleeping was impossible, especially when I needed to change positions. I called Dr. Halley. "I'm ready to schedule surgery."

It took a month to prepare for the hip replacement procedure, mainly because of all my other medical problems, and my work. Ed was there for me at every turn. He never got impatient or discouraged about our relationship. We didn't talk about marriage and we were both happy living in our separate homes. We were together every day we were both in town. His work took him all over the country. Occasionally we were in the same city on business. That was fun.

Three times before the surgery I had to give my own blood to the hospital through the Red Cross blood center. I read that hip replacements were messy...sort of like replacing one side of a wrecked car, and blood loss was plentiful. The losses had to be replaced by my own blood.

Dr. Halley explained that I would be fitted with a temporary pacemaker just before surgery to be removed just after surgery. This would not prevent me from going into atrial fib during the surgery but, because in regular rhythm my heart rate was so low—thirty-five beats per minute—the pacemaker would keep me at sixty beats per minute during surgery unless I went into A-Fib.

I was taken off the blood thinner a few days before scheduled surgery but would go back on it right after. I was taking another medication in the form of an injection to protect me from a blood clot and stroke. I didn't want to think about the dangerous things that could happen. I couldn't let myself think about them. Besides, the hip pain was so bad and walking was so difficult that I could only think about getting a new hip.

My sons, Mark and Brian, came in from Connecticut and Oregon to be in Columbus for the event. My sister was glad to have her nephews with us. We had to be at the hospital at five in the morning, though the surgery didn't take place until mid-afternoon. A nurse wrote on my thighs with a marker, "This leg" on the right one and "Not this leg" on the left. I was thankful for the strong pain medication and relaxer before going into the operating room. I didn't know a thing until it was all over.

It had to be less than twelve hours later that rehabilitation staff came in to get me up and walking. I was scared. I was put into a harness and hooked up to a strong young man who lifted me up and instructed me to walk. "Are both my legs the exact same length?" I asked. I had a dream that one leg would come out longer than the other. The nurse laughed and then I thought that if both hips could be replaced at one time, could they add an inch or two during surgery to make me taller?

The pain was gone. It was gone immediately. I had pain from the surgery and the seventy stitches down my leg and hip, but when I walked, the pain I had endured for the last six months was gone.

By the second day after walking several times down the hall and back to the room, assisted by the staff and hooked up with the harness, it was time to walk with minimum devices. Dr. Halley was pleased with the way surgery went and recovery was going. He did not want me to use a walker or wooden crutches. Instead, he said I could use one, just one, metal forearm crutch. I had to learn to do that. Full attention was needed because the crutch was under the arm on the opposite side of the hip that had just been replaced. It didn't seem natural. The progression was: place crutch in front of left hip (the good one) and step up to it with left leg placing weight there and bring right leg attached to new hip up to it. Then repeat. It was slow going, but it was going and without pain.

My sister Joan, a widow, had a comfortable home with a large master bedroom and two bathrooms on the first floor. She had a king size bed and she insisted I share it with her during my recovery so that she'd be close by day and night.

The most difficult part of recovery was sleeping on my back, something I never did. It would be weeks before I could sleep on my side, and then only on the side where the surgery had taken place and with a small pillow between my knees, something that I continued to do for a few months. Sleeping on my back was hard on the backs of my heels. They rubbed on the covers and sheets and became sore even wearing socks.

I started walking outside as soon as I got to my sister's house from the hospital. Within a week after the surgery I was walking a mile, slowly and with the assistance of my sister or Ed. Rehabilitation was only walking, no other exercise. I did notice that while lying flat on my back it was comfortable and natural to turn the recovering foot inward. After a short time I saw that when I walked, the recovering foot still turned inward. I had to concentrate on keeping that foot straight.

Joan took good care of me. She had a busy life and was gone to her various activities much of each day, especially on weekends and evenings. She did not want to leave me alone. She scheduled Ed and my friends to stay and she gave them careful instructions about what I could and could not do. Whenever I left the house she followed me out the door with further instructions and made sure I had my square pillow to sit on everywhere, keeping my hips above the knees. I started referring to her as Nurse Ratched—lovingly, of course.

The hip replacement worked out well. I had a few episodes of atrial fib, but the hip pain went away, stitches came out, I was walking perfectly though I used a cane for the last two weeks and had successfully conducted business for Bob without issue. Though I couldn't play a full round of golf, Ed drove me around the golf course and I managed to pitch and putt when we got close to the green.

The left hip was deteriorating quickly. One year after the first hip replacement, I scheduled the surgery for replacing that left hip knowing that the experience would be easy and soon I would be good as new. I was wrong.

CHAPTER SIX

1999

My vision was groggy and I couldn't focus on what should have been the recovery room. Too many people were in the background. I was lying flat on my back. I turned my head to hushed voices and immediately saw two figures in white staring down at me while another white-clothed figure hovered over my upper body.

"Am I dead?" I asked. "Where am I?"

"You're in the Intensive Care Unit (ICU) and you had a hip replacement," a female voice said.

The hovering figure was a nurse taking my vitals. The two others in white were doctors, one was Dr. Halley. The slighter and younger man next to him was holding a stethoscope. The others in the room moved closer to the bed. Ed and my sons stood next to me with worried looks on their faces.

The smaller doctor, an electrophysiologist as I learned later, spoke first, "After the surgery when we removed the temporary pacemaker, you went into atrial fib and your heart stopped for several seconds. Then it started up at a fast irregular pace and paused again for several seconds. You need a permanent pacemaker and it needs to be implanted right away."

"When?" I asked.

"Tomorrow or day after," Dr. Halley said, "but you can't get out of bed until it's in."

My head was clearing but I wasn't panicked. I knew there were pauses of several seconds when I went into atrial fib. I had told that to Dr. Caldwell, but I knew that they were only a couple of seconds and would start up again. I hadn't been scared but maybe I should have been. Besides, I wasn't at my hospital, The Ohio State University Medical Center, because Dr. Halley operated only at Riverside Methodist Hospital, an equally large major medical center. Riverside Methodist didn't have my detailed medical records except for what had been given to them before both hip replacements. Could they be overreacting?

"But Dr. Halley, what about getting me up to start rehab on this left hip?" I asked. "If I don't get up and start moving, that muscle could atrophy, couldn't it? Then, wouldn't I be left with a limp?" I was whining, but for good reason. It was my theory that if I did everything right during recovery and walked religiously, I could build up that muscle in my legs and hips protecting and strengthening the area encasing the hips to last forever. Maybe, eventually, I could cross my legs, a habit that had been hard to break after the first hip replacement. By the time my second hip was ready for surgery, I had a walking schedule of four or five miles, three to four days a week. Was I obsessed?

"A week or even longer won't affect your recovery," said Dr. Halley. "Concentrate on getting a pacemaker and good heart health right now."

The ICU room where I was lying flat on my back was crowded with family, doctors and a nurse who was trying to rid the room of so many people. Another visitor entered. Ed went to greet his friend Walter who had checked the hospital about my condition after the "routine" hip replacement and discovered my current situation.

"Hi, Walter. How'd you get into the ICU?" Ed asked.

"I just told them at the desk that I was one of Rosalie's ex-husbands and they directed me here." Everybody laughed. "How are you doing?" he asked, coming over next to Ed at my bedside.

"Not as good as you are," I said.

"Thanks, Walter," Ed said. "We needed a laugh." Walter stayed for a couple of minutes then Ed walked him out to the hall while my orthopedic surgeon, Dr. Halley, explained that I would be moved to the coronary unit of the hospital in preparation for the procedure to insert a pacemaker in my chest.

The electrophysiologist spoke with an Asian accent, which was difficult to understand in my present half-awake condition. Alert enough, I asked, "How will the move to the heart floor affect initial recovery of my hip? Is the staff there able to care for my hip problems while I wait for the pacemaker, or even while I recover from a second surgery within a two day period?"

I think I was asking the right questions, but maybe not getting the right answers. Ed came back in the room while I waited for an answer to, "What will take precedence, the pacemaker surgery or the recovery from the hip replacement?" The two doctors looked at each other and I felt that I had to take an active part in the next step of my predicament.

The electrophysiologist explained that the pacemaker procedure was not open heart surgery. "Most patients go home within twenty-four hours. You'll be given medication to relax and make you sleepy, but you will be awake. We make a two inch incision here," he said, touching my upper left chest, "attach one or two lead wires through the veins and insert the small device. Then we will program the pacemaker, close the incision with a couple of stitches, test it to make sure it is working correctly and that it will meet the needs you require."

"Which are?" I asked.

"The pacemaker keeps your heart rate from going too low. In regular rhythm you are at thirty-five beats per minute, which is quite low. When you are in atrial fib, you could go to two hundred or more beats per minute. From what we witnessed when we removed the temporary pacemaker after hip replacement, the irregularity caused pauses and stoppages. If we set the pacemaker at sixty beats per minute, you won't go lower than that, but it doesn't mean that you won't go higher than sixty. To answer your question, you will probably still go into atrial fibrillation. You will, however, be safer."

I couldn't absorb any more information. The hip was hurting from the surgery. The nurse offered pain medication. "What medication specifically," I asked. I didn't get along well with anything that had codeine in it.

"I'll give you a shot of Dilaudid," she said. The medication was put into the IV hooked up to the vein in my arm. Before it began to take effect, Mark and Brian said they were going to dinner with their Aunt Joan and Ed. I asked where they were going, but I was asleep before I could hear their answer.

The next morning tests were taken for the upcoming procedure. I was moved out of the ICU to the heart wing.

Ed and Walter played tennis every Friday with their friend Bud, a cardiologist in a group that worked out of Riverside Methodist Hospital. He heard of my dilemma and stopped by to check on me. Bud was my salvation those few days before and after the pacemaker insertion. I was suffering from desertion, fear and claustrophobia in a crowded double room. When Bud came through the flimsy gray curtain drawn around my bed, he lightened my frustrations as my friend, not my doctor. I felt old and depressed, maybe because I thought that a pacemaker was surely a sign of being decrepit.

I was partially awake for the insertion of the pacemaker, though I felt no pain. Follow-up care was simple, especially since I would be extra careful taking care of the hip. I tested my heart rate checking on my new body part to see if it changed me. It did. I felt less tired. When not in A-Fib, a heart rate of thirty-five beats per minute is debilitating. Now at sixty beats per minute I felt revived, not decrepit at all.

Before being discharged back to the orthopedic wing to start rehabilitation on the hip, I met with the electrophysiologist and requested that all records having to do with the pacemaker be sent to The Ohio State University Medical Center. They were in charge of my heart problems and that's the way I wanted it. I was taking control of my body and would learn all I could to maintain its future use and longevity. When it came to reading and listening to those who knew what would work best for my body, I questioned everything.

I carried the square pillow everywhere with me for longer than necessary to make sure my hips were always above my knees until I was sure the new hip was healed. My philosophy was that a little inconvenience could mean a lifetime of comfort.

CHAPTER SEVEN
2000

It's wonderful to live in an age when people can have their body parts replaced. I had two new hips that worked perfectly. I could do everything except cross my legs. Dr. Halley said, "Maybe someday, in the future." Since my job involved going through airport security at least twice each week, it was necessary to announce that I had metal hip replacements and a pacemaker. I was asked to show the card the hospital gave me proving that I had a pacemaker. I can't imagine why someone would lie about that, but eventually I just didn't tell security about the device in my chest, unless it set off an alarm.

I didn't tell security about my metal hips either unless they, too, set off the alarm. Usually they didn't, and I walked right through unannounced. After a while I took note of which airports had security turned up to where my hips and/or pacemaker would set off the metal detector. In the Columbus, Ohio airport, only Terminal C's security detected my interior metal. I asked Dr. Caldwell if it was a danger to me and my pacemaker going through security. "No," she said, "but if they use a wand on you, tell them you have a pacemaker and not to get the magnetic wand near your heart." The few times that happened, I was reprimanded by the security staff that I should announce my pacemaker ahead of time. I never did.

When I changed my pacemaker records to The Ohio State University Medical Center from Riverside Methodist, another electrophysiologist, Dr. Charles Love, was assigned to deal with my pacemaker. Dr. Caldwell was still my cardiologist.

I was issued a telephone transmission kit that contained a cradle for a land-line telephone receiver, a donut-size magnet and two arm bands, each with a metal plate to touch damp soft skin on the insides of my arms. These fit halfway up my arm between wrist and elbow and they connected to the transmission device with different colored wires. I was notified by mail as to the exact time of the test and precisely at that moment the phone would ring and I was told to begin the test. The person at the other end was real, not a computer generated voice, and if I wasn't ready, she would politely wait until I was. I'd be asked to put the magnet at my chest and the phone in the cradle of the device and wait thirty seconds for each of two or three tests. I could feel my heart pacemaker slow way down, then go fast. Sometimes the slow test made me dizzy. Then the voice at the other end of the phone would tell me all was working and approximately how much battery life was left. The whole test lasted less than five minutes.

Twice each year I went to the pacemaker clinic at the hospital for a more complete test with Dr. Love, in person. I was told that the life of the pacemaker was six to ten years, and that rather than change batteries they would update with the newest model. The lead wires would be tested and used for all future pacemaker insertions if they were still good. That way the procedure to change the device would be less invasive.

Currently, I am wearing a second pacemaker. This one has many more features than the first one. For example, when I'm in atrial fibrillation, the pacemaker records each episode, date, time and length. It does practically everything except cook dinner, but I don't do that either.

My first visit with Dr. Love was under different circumstances from a normal doctor/ patient visit. He sat at a complicated looking computer with hook ups for wires and recorders. I sat in a chair that reclined. A young man in his forties, Dr. Love explained what he was doing and asked if I had questions. I did. I felt comfortable talking to him about anything. He was open and had a sense of humor.

"Dr. Love, are there any restrictions? Can I exercise, sleep on my stomach and continue the things I do now?" I asked.

"No restrictions, but for the next two months limit the amount of weight you carry to ten pounds and use your right arm to lift and carry, not left," he said. "Do you have a mobile phone?" he asked. I nodded. "Use your right ear, farther away from your heart rather than left."

"Is there anything that I will never be able to do?"

"With today's pacemakers, you should not have an MRI (magnetic resonance imaging)," he said.

He explained that an MRI was a radiology scan, a technique that uses radio waves and a computer to produce images of the body. I didn't get it but figured that it had something to do with the magnets used in the telephone transmissions and tests he was setting up. Maybe magnets interfered with pacing mechanisms. I had a vision of my pacemaker connected to my body colliding with the MRI capsule, stuck together in a magnetic field of metal.

"I had an MRI before each of my hip replacement surgeries. What if I'd need one for something else?" I asked.

"You can have a CT scan for the chest, abdomen or pelvis," he said. "That's a 3-D x-ray. New inventions in medicine and imaging are happening every day."

It wouldn't be too many months before I would be faced with another imaging decision.

"How is the heart rate fixed for the pacemaker? Do you decide?" I asked.

Dr. Love checked the pacing rate. "The setting is at sixty beats per minute right now."

"Is that standard? Or, can you set it higher? I was at thirty-five for so long and I walked around tired all the time. Everything was an effort. Can you set it at seventy beats per minute?"

"I can," he said. "Do you think that'll help your golf game?"

"Exactly!" I said.

§

By the time we entered the new millennium and said goodbye to the twentieth century, I was feeling good. I was walking a fifteen-minute mile on the treadmill or outside, averaging four miles three or four days a week. The heart rate at seventy beats per minute made a positive difference in my energy level, except for the days and hours I was in A-Fib when it was so fast and irregular that I couldn't get a count. Lack of oxygen made any movement difficult. The A-Fib impact became worse. I realized that after completing the necessary work-related tasks, I needed to rest and do nothing. I was long past being scared of having a stroke. I just wanted the A-Fib to end forever.

I read more and more about the frequency of the aging population suffering from A-Fib. Now there were more doctors and clinics throughout the country performing the heart ablation. One of the doctors at the Cleveland Clinic was renowned for this procedure. However, Dr. Caldwell wasn't sure the ablation was to be taken seriously yet.

In the year 2000, the cardiac ablation was defined as a procedure that can correct heart rhythm problems using long, flexible tubes (catheters) inserted through a vein in the groin and threaded to the heart. The ablation can correct problems in the heart's electrical system that cause an arrhythmia. Still new, it had been performed on patients not responding to medications for atrial fibrillation.

Meanwhile, in February of that year, Ed was commissioned to give a speech at the Young Presidents Organization (YPO) conference in Australia. As his significant other, I was invited to go along. This was my second trip to Australia, the first being ten years previously. I had been in atrial fib during the entire time.

This time Ed and I were guests of YPO. We were in Sydney less than a week but I never recovered from jet lag. The time difference of fourteen hours plus the sixteen hour flight kept my body jet lagged for two weeks after returning to the

United States. I was in atrial fib for most of that time too. I was a mess.

My work schedule changed as the company added more regional sales people. Howie covered the East Coast, Roger was in the South, Phil ran the West Coast sales office and I was in charge of the Midwest from Pittsburgh to Denver and Minneapolis to Bentonville, Arkansas. All of us, except Howie who worked from the New Jersey headquarters office, operated the business from our homes and traveled Tuesdays through Thursdays. If I went to a city within 200 miles of Columbus, I drove. Otherwise I flew and usually rented a car at my destination.

The company had started a new line of heart-healthy margarines. At first they were called Heart Beat. Then we changed it to Smart Beat and finally to Smart Balance. Our manufacturers used a variety of healthy oils and fats, but the processes used to make these products made them taste better and eliminated partially hydrogenated oils, substances that made margarines unhealthy. Besides being healthy, Smart Balance tastes like butter.

My job continued as spokesperson and salesperson for Smart Balance margarine and other items not part of that line of foods. When I traveled to a city, I worked with the food broker and his staff of sales people who visited the individual grocery stores to make sure the foods they represented were placed correctly on the shelves according to a computerized plan of operation. Pricing, number of shelf facings and fresh rotations were important. Often I would call a meeting of all company salespeople and educate them about our products and what we expected their sales staff to do. Broker managers who called on buyers at supermarket chain headquarters took me with them when I visited their city. I presented new items, special promotions and our upcoming advertising schedules hoping to get stores to advertise and display our items.

I loved my job though it filled my life with plenty of stress from the stores, the food brokers and my boss. Sometimes a customer deducted from their payment to us an unauthorized amount of money, or they were slow in paying the bill altogether. It was my job to get paid in full and on time. This led to even more stress.

So, when I went to Omaha in late March of the year 2000, I had a return ticket to fly back on Thursday afternoon of that week. I didn't come home until Sunday.

CHAPTER EIGHT
APRIL 2000

Sitting on the edge of the examining table, I was eight inches higher than Dr. Caldwell who had moved her round backless seat on wheels over to me. She was holding a report and the DVD of my heart attack and catheterization from Omaha less than one week before.

My sister Joan was in the room too.

"How are you feeling today, Mrs. Linver?"

"I wish I felt better than I do. Maybe it's just because I'm scared. What did the doctors in Omaha report?" I asked, indicating the DVD and file she held in her hand.

"You have a single blocked artery. The left anterior descending artery is one of three major arteries in the heart, and it's blocked more than fifty percent," she said.

"I just don't understand it," I said shaking my head. "The cholesterol tests I've had don't show excessively high cholesterol. I eat right, and exercise. What is the blockage from?"

"Don't forget that genetically you have history. Didn't both of your parents die from heart disease?"

"Yes," I said, "but they were a lot older than I am now."

"The blockage is not just cholesterol. That artery is full of 'junk,'" she said.

"What do you mean, 'junk'?"

"Calcium and other non-soft material could have been accumulating for years, maybe even since you were a teenager." She went on, "It appears that a piece chipped off into the bloodstream and caused your heart attack."

"What if more pieces chip off?" I asked.

"We'll watch it, and I want to see you back here in a week. Call me before that if you don't feel better. Have you been in A-Fib?"

"Yes," I said, "but not for more than a couple of hours. I woke up with it this morning but went back to regular rhythm after two hours. I'm trying not to think of anything stressful. Would the stress from the heart attack cause me to feel so tired?"

"Possibly," she said. "Try not to do much before I see you again."

The following day I felt better and Ed and I went to our favorite restaurant for dinner, The Top Steak House, an upscale, long-time Columbus tradition from the 1950s. Authentically retro, The Top had special meaning for us because we had been introduced and *fixed-up* by Sonia who commanded the piano bar and kept the music going all evening long. She hosted a gang of would-be singers who sometimes brought a file box of words to hundreds of songs that Sonia could play in any key. Her piano separated the *Cheers* type bar from the dining room lined with black leather booths, a few tables and dimmed lights reminiscent of a black and white movie in the 1950s.

Sonia loved to put people together. She knew Ed and how unhappy he had been when he became single again. She had known me for years, even before I moved back to Columbus from Europe and California. I had been single for nine years and she'd say to me each time I came to listen at one of the restaurants where she had followers, "One of these days, Rosalie, I'm going to find someone for you." And, she did. When Ed and I got married in 2001, Sonia played the piano at our wedding. She announced to everyone that we were her thirty-sixth match to marry.

After dinner at The Top that night, Ed went home and I went to bed, but not for long. Around midnight I woke up with pains in my left shoulder and arm. I didn't want to bother

Ed, but I knew that my cousin Sandra would still be up and so would her husband, Jerry, my pharmacist. I called them. Jerry asked Sandra to come over and stay with me.

Sandra arrived and insisted she take me to the hospital emergency room, a five-minute drive. This, however, was not The Ohio State University Hospital, which was farther away. When we arrived at the emergency room and I went to registration, the woman in charge asked me why I didn't call 911. How dumb could I be? This was my second trip to an emergency room in a week and both times I had been scolded about not calling 911. It could have been a more pleasant evening for my cousin Sandra if I had done so.

As it turned out, I spent five or six hours at the ER. Sandra stayed the whole time. I underwent a lot of tests again. They decided I should be admitted to OSU. Poor Sandra was so tired. Finally, as it was starting to get light outside, she went home and I went to OSU Hospital by ambulance.

It's a funny thing about a teaching hospital, or maybe it's only The OSU Hospital; the clinic doctors that I had seen in their offices away from the actual hospital did not visit their patients once they were admitted as in-patients. Once I was assigned to a room in the main hospital, I didn't see Dr. Caldwell again until all procedures for this problem were over. A different staff of cardiologists visited me and conducted sessions with an entourage of students, interns and residents. I felt like I had lost some control over my body. Dr. Caldwell and I had good rapport. We understood each other. I had a confidence in her that I'm sure she could feel. Without her, I would have to restructure body management.

My sons, Mark and Brian, came from Connecticut and Oregon. Ed spent a lot of time at the hospital. His office was not far away. My sister was there, as was my niece, Lisa, and a variety of friends. My boss, Bob, and his wife and sons were on the phone talking to everyone: doctors, relatives and me. The consensus of the docs was that I needed an operation to bypass that left anterior descending artery, open heart surgery. Shit! Why was this happening? Panic was not good for me. I had to settle down. Thousands of people went through this. Why me? Why not me?

How were the heart attack and the upcoming bypass surgery connected to my now more than twenty-year history and affliction with atrial fibrillation? I was told by a variety of heart doctors who made rounds that there was no connection. Strange that both problems involved the same organ and had very little to do with one another. The A-Fib was being treated with amiodarone, an anti-arrhythmia drug that didn't work all of the time. How would it and the blood thinner, warfarin, react to the surgery? Surely, I would be on some other blood thinning medication to prevent blood pool and stroke. How did the less than year old pacemaker fit in? The upper left side of my body was a busy place.

Feeling sorry for myself, I deserved the gush of tears I let go. Without witnesses I could cry as much as I wanted, especially when I realized that open heart surgery was just that—opened heart. Doctors actually stop the heart and pass the blood through a heart-lung machine while the operation is being performed. For bypass surgery the heart itself is not opened up. The ugly chest scar I saw on people when they wore open collar shirts or low cut blouses was just part of the evidence that they had survived a miracle operation. My brother-in-law didn't survive it in 1979, but that was twenty-one years before. So much progress had been made, and I would soon be a witness to some of it.

Thursday afternoon Ed and I watched the first day of the Masters Golf Tour from my hospital room. I was not allowed out of bed, I guess for fear of shaking up the blockage in my artery and breaking off another chip of "junk." It was late in the day for an entourage of doctors to make rounds, but a small group of three men headed by a fit and confident, almost arrogant-looking, fortyish hunk, walked in briskly and stood at the end of my bed.

"Mrs. Linver, I am Doctor Randall Wolf, cardiothoracic

surgeon." He went on to introduce the other two doctors he brought with him. I introduced all of them to Ed. The two doctors with Dr. Wolf looked more mature than the students and interns that I had seen previously.

"We've studied your cardiac history and your recent heart attack and know that you are scheduled for heart bypass surgery," he said. I grabbed both sides of the bed frame bracing myself for bad news. "From what I have observed, Mrs. Linver, you are a good candidate for a less invasive surgical procedure that would solve your problem without the more invasive open heart bypass surgery. You are a good candidate because you have a single blockage and its location is in the artery that is easy to reach robotically."

Just then I had a vision of a movie I had seen many years before, *Fantastic Voyage,* a science fiction thriller starring Raquel Welch and Stephen Boyd. A crew of doctors were miniaturized and sent through the bloodstream of a human body in a tiny boat. I'd forgotten the story until just that moment. It gave a whole new meaning to blood vessel.

Dr. Wolf continued to explain his totally endoscopic cardiac surgery and that he was at The Ohio State University for a short time to do this procedure. He also traveled, teaching endoscopic coronary bypass all over the world. "We will make two incisions, between these two ribs and a small incision under the left breast." He showed Ed and me exactly where. "Eventually the scars from the two incisions will completely fade."

"How long will I be in the hospital?" I asked.

"Two days, possibly less."

I told him that I would let him know the following day as I wanted to discuss it with my sons and other family members. He agreed but then told me that the surgery would have to take place on Monday because he was scheduled out of the city the rest of that week. What I really wanted to do was check out his credentials and references.

Dr. Wolf's bio was impressive as was the one reference I was able to check on such short notice. Robotic surgeries were becoming more and more popular, but not so much with the heart. However, an article we found online about Dr. Wolf described his minimally invasive technique, *In 1999, Dr. Randall Wolf of Cincinnati became the first U.S. surgeon to perform a coronary bypass using the da Vinci robotic surgical system. But he left Cincinnati so he could use the system at The Ohio State University Medical Center.* Most of his patients were men. I may have been the first woman in Columbus to have the endoscopic cardiac surgery.

"Can I go home for the weekend?" I asked.

"I'm afraid not. We don't even want you out of bed. You

will be moved to a room in the main hospital."

"What exactly are you going to be doing," I asked, "after you make the two incisions?"

He drew a diagram on the back of my menu. "We'll tie off and bypass the blocked left anterior descending artery with this mammary artery," he said as he made a few more gestures with his pen.

After he left, Ed, who had his computer on his lap, showed me some write-ups about Dr. Wolf and a series of photos. Most interesting, however, was that he was a practicing magician and a member of The Academy of Magical Arts (Magic Castle), which I had visited in Hollywood, California.

My new weekend retreat in the main part of The Ohio State University Hospital was awesome. Though it was one of the older rooms, it was spacious and private and had a nighttime lightshow view of downtown Columbus from my sixth floor window.

A steady stream of visitors kept me from thinking too much. Ed's good friend Walter and his wife, Mary Elizabeth, were up to their tricks, coming in Saturday with bags of stuff that they spread out on the indented desktop/dressing table against a mirrored wall. They started unpacking the bag that contained empty beer cans, wine bottles and even an empty vodka bottle. The matching plastic drinking ware had the look of being well used and even had lipstick stains in the right places. They littered it all over like there had been a big party in the room and with the mirror behind, it looked even grander. Nurses, doctors and aides got a charge out of it and sent others to the room to gawk.

Sunday was quiet and more or less a prep day for Monday's surgery. Besides wishing the surgery was over, I wished I could have washed my hair. The little things like that kept me from worrying about the bigger things like heart surgery.

Brian and Ed and my sister Joan walked my gurney to the operating room where a nurse had me get off the gurney and onto the operating table. First, though, the nurse guided me onto a scale. I never liked getting weighed. It was always such a disappointment. Not this time. The nurse noted my weight and announced, "It's nice to see a patient of normal weight." That's the last dialogue I heard until the surgery was over.

Recovery was relatively easy. I was home, up and about in two days. Lisa stayed with me for a week.

Shortly after the bypass, Ed and I were at Easton Center, an upscale shopping and restaurant area not far from New Albany where Ed lived. We had eaten dinner and were shopping at the Barnes & Noble book store near the restaurant when we saw Dr. Randall Wolf buying a book. I recognized him before he remembered me. He seemed so pleased to see me. Saving one's life is never to be taken for granted.

CHAPTER NINE

2000

When faced with a life-and-death crisis, some people crumble. That's what I had heard. It didn't make sense to me because I thought that if one faced death and recovered, then one should feel good about missing what could have been a tragedy. I guess we have no control over such emotions. I didn't know what I was feeling, but after the heart attack and bypass, my actions took on a new twist.

Recovery from the robotic bypass was not completely free of complications. A week after I came home from the hospital, during the middle of the night, my lungs became water balloons. I thought my chest would burst. I couldn't breathe. My niece had gone back home, and Ed was staying with me. The only comfort I found was to sit straight up in bed. I moved to the guest bedroom so I wouldn't wake up Ed, but within a few minutes he called out to me from where he was sleeping and rushed into my room. We quickly dressed and Ed took me to the emergency room at the nearest hospital. In my mind, I thought I might have a collapsed lung, but didn't think I would die.

X-rays showed that there was fluid in my chest. The ER doctor thought they would have to eliminate it by sticking a needle into my lungs. First though, they would try a large dose of diuretics. A portable toilet was rolled next to my bed in the ER. I went from bed to toilet and back to bed. This went on for two hours. I peed like someone was hosing me down. Seven pounds of water later I felt like a new woman. A prescription for diuretics in hand, Ed and I left the hospital at the same time the ER doctor went off duty. He spoke to us in the parking lot and told us that we made his day. "You were the only success I had on my shift," he said. "Now I can go home and happily go to sleep."

"You made my day, too," I said. Then I realized what could have happened. With all my health problems, I didn't seriously think I would die. Rather, my feelings were to just get the problem fixed without enduring a lot of physical pain. I was happy for the doctor that I didn't die on his watch.

It takes time to recover from robotic surgery, but not as long as if I'd had the open heart procedure. I stayed home. After another week I was able to drive. I didn't want to. I didn't want to do anything, but I did manage my business from the office in my condominium. I was tired from the surgery and the ordeal of the heart attack, being away from home three or four days a week, catching planes and staying in hotels. The bouts of atrial fib didn't let up. I had good days and I had bad ones. On a good day I had energy, a clear head and felt like accomplishing something—anything, even a walk or talking to one or more of the twenty food brokers I managed. I wrote sales plans, sent emails and made social arrangements with Ed and other friends. Bad days usually involved atrial fib, waking up tired and short of breath for several hours or the whole day.

I didn't know why but I decided that I needed to change my life and make it simpler. Owning a home or condo was a lot of responsibility and work. My condo was not small, almost 3,000 square feet. I certainly could live in less and not be tied to owning something that would keep me from moving away. In earlier times I enjoyed the freedom of not being attached to things and people. What was holding me here? The answer was easy and it was depressing…atrial fib, heart damage, two artificial hips, a pacemaker and thyroid problems. What next?

I told Ed that I wanted to put my condo up for sale. I even

looked at rental apartments not far from where I was living. Ed talked me out of selling. "You've just come through a rough time. Don't make any major decisions for a while." I heard him, but I didn't listen.

My boss, Bob, met me in Cincinnati for an appointment with a major grocery chain a few weeks after my heart bypass surgery. "You're looking good," he said. "I need you to get back to traveling and seeing customers one-on-one."

"I can't do it every week yet. I'll travel by car within two hundred miles for a few weeks longer and contact buyers and brokers by phone and email, but I'm not ready to fly, carry luggage, rent cars and start the lonely life of hotels and restaurants. Sales have been good. We haven't lost any business," I pleaded.

"I thought you liked the travel and all that goes with it," he said.

"Yes, I like it, but right now my body doesn't. Six weeks ago, Bob, I was staying in a Residence Inn Hotel in Omaha, Nebraska, an hour before I had a heart attack. I could have died, only to have had my body found by the maid who cleaned the room, maybe hours later."

He didn't get it.

Maybe it was I who didn't get it. I couldn't get back up on the horse after falling off. "Bob, maybe this life isn't for me."

"What are you saying?" he asked.

"I don't want to do this anymore," I said. "I'm giving you three months' notice to find someone to fill my job. I can't take this stress."

There! I did it. Bob coughed and stuttered and said we would talk later. I took him to the Cincinnati airport in silence so he could fly back to LaGuardia. I drove back to Columbus not realizing what I had just done. For more than twenty-three years I had worked for Bob and his family-owned little company that grew into a business sold to a major conglomerate for so much money that I couldn't even count the zeros. I was his first employee and remained the only one for five years. He always told me that I was family. Now he had started another business and I was part of it too. I had worked for Bob longer, by far, than I had been with any of my husbands.

I would find something else less stressful. I must. At age sixty-three I had to find a new career or job that would pay my insurance. It was almost two years before I could be on Medicare. I had medical problems with pre-conditions. How could I qualify for benefits? Who would hire me? Medical insurance became an obsession. It was that way for most people who could retire at age sixty-two but who could not have paid government insurance for three more years.

Bob didn't tell anyone that I quit. Maybe he told Cecily,

his wife. I don't know for sure. I only told Ed. Bob asked me not to tell any of the brokers I managed or people in the industry of co-workers or ask any of them for job leads. I promised I wouldn't, which meant I had to start cold. He reminded me that I had signed a non-compete contract saying that I would not work for any competitive company in the food industry for a limited amount of time.

First, I put a new resume together and went to a professional for the finished product. I hadn't updated my resume for twenty-five years or more. Though I had quit my job with Bob twice before during the twenty-three years, we always made up, and in the past I came out ahead financially. This was not the case now. I wanted to change my life, or I thought I did.

From June until mid-August I threw myself into looking for a new job. If nothing else, the search kept me from feeling sorry for myself and thinking about my health problems. I knew I could sell anything, tangible or intangible, as long as I believed in the product. My age was a detriment, though employers and agencies weren't allowed to discriminate. Because I was two years away from Medicare, I figured that some companies would be glad to get me off their health care books while I still had at least a decade of work energy left and a lot of experience. Those were positive thoughts until atrial fib would kick in and remind me, with a rapid heartbeat that now gave me a headache as well as shortness of breath, that I had pre-conditions for any new health care plan.

Bob was very pleasant to me that summer. We didn't see each other. He was in the New Jersey office, and I was either on the road in one of my markets or in my condo working in Columbus. We did talk on the phone at least once a day, sometimes three or four times. "How's the job search going?" he asked.

"I've had a few bites. Nothing serious," I answered.

"What are you looking for?" he asked.

"Well, Bob, I'd really like to find something like the job I have now."

"So why don't you stop looking and just stay?"

I really wanted to do just that, but I didn't want to sound as anxious as I felt. I didn't want to give him any conditions. I knew he didn't react well to conditions. So, I just said, "OK, I will." So much for being over anxious.

I don't want to appear as though between the beginning of feeling atrial fib and the year 2000, more than twenty years, I was sickly or I went through life scared of dying. For the most part, I did the things I wanted to do and I lived a normal and productive life. I felt safe with the blood thinner keeping me from stroking and the amiodarone reducing, though not eliminating, episodes of atrial fib. I wasn't naïve about its dangers, but when I felt my body go into the weird heartbeat that went with a number of side effects, I uttered under my breath, "Shit!" Then, instead of fighting it, I did what I had to do until I could rest. If I was in an airport or exercising or working, I slowed my mind and body, sipped from a bottle of water and never complained to anyone, not even my boss, Bob.

When I wasn't in A-Fib, I went full steam. Toward the end of 2000 after the November presidential election, Ed and I planned a trip to France. I had lived in France in 1974, and now, from traveling in my job, I had thousands of frequent flyer miles, enough for Ed and me to fly first class round trip and use thousands more for a plush hotel in Paris. Spending hours on the phone with the airlines, I could get us to Paris from Columbus, but I couldn't get us home. The only place in Europe we could fly free and first class to the U.S. was from Lisbon, Portugal.

I called Ed at work. "Have you been to Portugal?"

"No," he said. "Why?"

"We can only fly home free on TWA from Lisbon. Let's go there from Paris by train."

§

After four wonderful days in Paris and an overnight train ride through the mountains in Spain, we arrived on a sunny

November Portuguese morning. Three days seaside in beautiful Lisbon, a city that resembles San Francisco, brought us face-to-face with the history of their April 25, 1974, Carnation Revolution. I had been in Lisbon that day in 1974, witnessing a bloodless coup that overthrew a government in power for fifty years. It was an adventure then, but after leaving Lisbon, I never heard about the coup or that country's problems again.

The trip to Portugal twenty-six years before was part of a year-long adventure that included a lifetime of new friends. One, a handsome Portuguese Navy officer named Eduardo, I met the day of the coup amid all the celebrations in Lisbon. I don't know which event was more spectacular, experiencing the coup and all it had to offer, or the dashing Eduardo. I was currently experiencing flashbacks of both.

Memories of Portugal's 1974 coup made current American politics even more interesting for me. The U.S. presidential election of 2000 was still not settled when Ed and I went to Europe. Democratic candidate Al Gore and Republican candidate George W. Bush were in a tie. The election results were delayed for several weeks, complicated by counting and recounting votes in Florida, a swing state. The outcome was to be decided by intense vote counting and the U.S. Supreme Court. Hanging chads and a publicity-seeking Florida Secretary of State gained worldwide attention. Everywhere we went, especially in Lisbon where American tourists were few, we were asked, "Who will be president of the United States?"

We loved talking to the local residents and enjoyed the sense of humor of the Portuguese people. Ed and I were on opposite sides of the U.S. political spectrum so it was interesting to see the amusement the Portuguese showed when they discovered that Ed voted for one candidate and I voted for the other.

On the bus ride going to the airplane, our escort said to Ed, "Is this your first trip to Portugal?" Ed answered that it was his first trip, but that I had been here before.

I chimed in, "I was here on April 25, 1974."

"Oh," she said. "You were here on the day we gained our freedom."

"Yes, it was very exciting," I said. "I remember how happy the people were, dancing in the streets with parades and red carnations were everywhere. The people had been so poor and all the young men went to fight in the South African wars. The women had no men. Is it better now?" I asked.

"My brother went to Germany to stay out of war. That part is better, but the people are still poor. Nothing has really changed."

I reached into my purse and pulled out all the escudos I had and handed them to her, but she shook her head and refused to take them. "Please," I said. "Take them, I can't use them and besides, soon your country will be using euros and the escudos will be useless. At least you can use them now." She still wouldn't take them, and yes, Portugal's money is now the euro.

The night before we left for home I felt a cold coming on. My head and throat were hurting. We went to dinner in an elegant restaurant near our hotel. When we arrived, Ed asked if we could sit in the non-smoking section. "Yes, of course," we were told by the manager who moved an ashtray from a table that was surrounded by other tables with ashtrays. Almost everyone smoked in Lisbon. It reminded us of the 1950s at home. We laughed and imagined a declaration, "Welcome to Portugal where you must smoke."

My head blossomed into a cold and fever by the time we reached the airport, and even in a first class seat, I couldn't get comfortable. Before we boarded I bought nasal spray and antihistamines to relieve the congestion. I wiped my runny eyes to check directions and disclaimers on the packaging before swallowing or spraying anything. "Do not use if you have heart problems or thyroid disease," was boldly printed on the containers. I had both. I took them anyway.

How did I feel being back in a country I'd heard nothing about for twenty-six years? I felt sad that very little had changed there, but so much had happened to me, most of it good in spite of my health issues.

Yep, I was back to reality, but I didn't have any episodes of A-Fib during the vacation, that I know of. A full week of feeling normal. I liked it.

CHAPTER TEN

2001

"Are you familiar with Reiki, Rosalie?" Jodi asked. My friend Jodi was a psychotherapist who dealt with alternative therapies and natural medications, usually derived from herbs. We had been discussing my bouts of atrial fib and the frustrations I felt not being able to control them. Besides, the frequency of the episodes was causing disruption in my daily living even more now.

"No, what's Reiki?"

"It's a Japanese technique for stress reduction that promotes healing and is administered by a practitioner or teacher by 'laying on hands,'" she said.

"What do you mean, 'laying on hands'?" I had visions of

me lying on my hands or someone else's hands or someone lying on my hands.

"It's based on the idea that unseen life force energy flows through us. It's what causes us to be alive. If one's life energy force is low," Jodi explained, "we may get sick or feel stress. High life energy force promotes good health and happiness. The 'laying on hands' means that the practitioner's hands will touch points that distribute energy and harmony. Sometimes the practitioner will not touch the body, but the hands will hover an inch or two above it."

"Can it help me diminish the bouts of atrial fib?" I asked.

"I don't think it can rid you of it, but it can help relieve your stress. Can't hurt, anyway. Body harmony and energy fields can direct a lot of healing," she said. "If you are interested, I have a friend who does Reiki and takes patients in her home. She lives in South Bexley. I'll give you her number and you can talk to her."

I called her. Spring was coming and I was desperate to seek help. I spoke to Jodi's friend Allison who promised nothing, but suggested I try Reiki for one session. We made a Friday morning appointment for ten o'clock. She had children who would be in school. Concentration and peaceful surroundings were important, I surmised.

Bexley is an upscale part of the Columbus area. Allison

lived in an older middle class neighborhood with two-story homes surrounded by lots of trees in bloom with sweet smelling blossoms promising a lush spring and summer. Inside she ushered me up the center hallway steps to a tidy and colorful room that she had converted from bedroom to office where she saw patients. Through the screens and open windows one could hear the branches sway in the gentle breeze and watch as the pink and white blossoms dropped pastel confetti to the ground like snow. We talked softly about my A-Fib, and she explained her technique. She didn't touch, but her hands hovered an inch or two from the areas affected by my problem. The room, the air, the sound of the trees and the sunshine all contributed to the feeling of contentment and well-being. This went on for forty minutes with her speaking gently from time-to-time. When finished, I felt like I had been in a coma coming out totally relaxed and happy.

She asked, without pressure, how I felt and did I want to make another appointment.

"Yes," I said. "How about two weeks from today?"

I kept going every other Friday at ten o'clock for a few months. No, it didn't help my atrial fib, but I was always anxious to go and I felt good in and after the Reiki sessions. When the trees were rich with leaves, I particularly loved hearing the noises from the quiet neighborhood. Allison never closed her windows and we never needed air conditioning. Once she gave me a smooth royal blue glass object the size of a dime. "When you go into A-Fib, hold it in your hand and rub it gently between your thumb and index finger." I did, and it always made me feel calm even while the crazy heart rhythm was fluttering. The tiny disc is still in my desk drawer staring at me like a sapphire, reminding me of contentment.

Though it didn't help my atrial fib, I have great respect for Reiki and the harmony it brought to me.

§

That summer of 2001 would have been perfect if not for A-Fib. My relationship with Ed was completing its fourth year. We weren't living together. His house was only five minutes away from mine. To everyone we knew, we were a couple, though marriage wasn't discussed. It didn't need to be.

Ed's house had been for sale over a year. Finally, it sold. Some of our friends and family thought he would move in with me, but it wasn't an issue for either of us. He invited me to join him and his realtor when he looked at other houses. I wasn't part of the decision, nor did I want to be, so I thought. We were both happy being independent and living alone, though when we were both in Columbus, we spent all of our time together. Ed bought a house in New Albany, a suburb where young families were building a fresh community. It was, however, at least twenty minutes by car from where I lived and the distance became an inconvenience.

Ed's prior relationship ended tragically a year before we started seeing each other. He and Pat had been together for over five years. After their first year together, Pat developed breast cancer. She was in her mid-forties. Ed nursed her through cancer until early in 1997 when she passed away. The cancer had spread to other parts of her body. During our four year courtship, I felt he never really recovered from losing her.

Ed's first marriage ended tragically too, but because he had three children (two teenagers and Elizabeth, a toddler) he was unable to grieve in a manner that would enable him to move on. So here he was, alone, having lost two women in his life, raising three children and managing a company of 3,000 employees.

I loved him, but was it fair to be part of his life not being a healthy person myself? After the heart attack, continuous battles with atrial fib, two hip replacements, pacemaker and other surgeries and procedures, didn't Ed deserve a woman in good health? Granted, cancer didn't run in my family, but there are no guarantees.

I had been married three times, never for more than six or seven years at a time. Here I was at age sixty-three with less than twenty years in marriage. I asked myself, what's wrong with me? And is it fair to marry this wonderful man and put him through more ill health and then die on him?

July 4th weekend that year brought Elizabeth and her husband, Jon, to Columbus for a visit from their home in Philadelphia. Ed's son, Mark, and his family were joining us for a family cookout later that day. I was in Ed's kitchen. When I turned to him, he had one knee on the floor. I thought he had fallen. "What are you doing down there?" I asked.

"Calm down. I'm proposing marriage. Will you marry me?" he asked.

That was the start of something great. But when Ed tells the story of how he proposed to me, he says, "I proposed to her in my kitchen, and she hasn't been back since."

With some difficulty, because much of our family lived out of town, we decided to get married October 13 that year of 2001. A lot happened between July 4th weekend and October 13, but even what was not good was eclipsed by the happiness surrounding our wedding plans.

Atrial fib was always with me. During a regularly scheduled appointment with Dr. Caldwell, she told me that many changes were about to take place at The Ohio State University Medical Center. Most of them had to do with the Ross Heart Hospital, which was under construction and would be ready in less than two years. Research was being done on heart arrhythmias and The OSU Heart Medical Center was preparing to expand its electrophysiology department. She also told me that more research was being done on the use of the procedure called heart ablation to eliminate some forms of atrial fibrillation. Some ablation procedures were already being done at the Cleveland Clinic. She could see the excitement on my face. "I wouldn't plan on doing it yet, it's too new, but so much evidence and technology are available now that weren't available before," she said. "It gives us all hope that atrial fib can be eliminated for many patients in the future."

The travel part of my job continued with a flight almost every week to one or more of the twenty cities where my job took me. Sometimes I drove if the distance was within 200 miles. The driving weeks were fun because it was before digital cell phones, and though I had a mobile analog phone in the car, the service was spotty and not good for lengthy business calls. This allowed me drive-time for listening to books on tape, even before CDs were available in cars.

On the morning of September 11, before eight o'clock, I boarded a plane in Columbus for a non-stop flight to Minneapolis. We were scheduled to be in the air for an hour and forty minutes. Halfway to our destination the pilot announced that we would be making an unscheduled stop in Milwaukee, Wisconsin. He was quick to tell us that nothing was wrong with the plane.

"We've been told that there is a national emergency and that all aircraft currently in the air must land at the nearest major airport," he announced without hesitation. "That is all that I know at this time, but I will continue to update you as we approach Milwaukee within fifteen minutes."

I was sitting in a window seat and as I looked out of the window, I noticed an eerie lack of activity below. As we approached Milwaukee practically no cars could be seen from the air. Then, I saw a military vehicle, just one, below and I felt scared. The plane was not full and I heard another passenger tell his seat mate behind me that he had just called someone in New York (against the rules on a moving aircraft) and that a plane just crashed into the World Trade Center.

We landed in Milwaukee. Several other planes were circling waiting for the go-ahead to land.

"A gate agent will guide you off this plane and usher you into the main terminal," the pilot said. "You are not to stop until you reach the main area. Do not stop at the restrooms or stop to make any phone calls on the way. You are instructed to get your baggage and vacate the terminal."

As soon as the plane landed I telephoned Ed on my mobile phone. He told me what happened. All of the passengers were scurrying off the plane with carry-on baggage in one hand and phone in the other. "They think there are several planes in the air targeting other airports," Ed said. "One or two, they think, are on the way to Washington, D.C. Get out of there as soon as you can."

In the main terminal I stopped at a snack bar with a mounted TV. A crowd of people huddled looking up at a scene that could only be an action movie in black and white. We all gasped and some were crying, not just women, but men wiped their eyes in horror. I couldn't believe what I was seeing. I was watching a plane crash into a high rise building, then come out the other side on fire! Almost immediately it happened to the tall building next to the first one. The twin towers of the World Trade Center were being invaded by our own airplanes full of Americans burning inside them. I was shaking. I didn't have time to listen to more TV coverage. Decisions had to be made.

I can't go on to Minneapolis. How do I get home? Am I stuck in Milwaukee? I remembered that my friend Harriet lived in Milwaukee. If necessary, I figured I could go to her apartment about a half-hour ride from the airport. How would I get there? Maybe she would come and get me, though I could see from the panic in and around me that visitors would probably have a difficult time getting through. The conversation I was having with myself was calm, surprisingly reasonable in spite of the chaos.

Fortunately I had not checked luggage. My briefcase was strapped to the roll-on while my purse was secured in the other hand. I took the escalator down to rental car counters. The lines at each were long. I did have a Hertz car reserved in Minneapolis, but this was Milwaukee. Figuring the smaller car rentals would run out of cars soon, I got into the Hertz line. They, for sure, had more cars than the other agencies. Thirty-five people were in front of me. The line went all the way back to the escalator.

Then a young woman about thirty people ahead of me, stepped out of the line facing those waiting for cars and in a firm but shaky voice asked, "Is anyone going to Toledo or Northwest Ohio and would share a car with me?" I remembered seeing her on my plane so I knew she had been headed for Minneapolis.

I didn't even have to think about it. I raised my hand, stepped forward and said, "Yes. I will." She smiled as if relieved.

By now she was next in line. I offered to split the price of the rental car, the drop off fee and gas. She said that her company would pay for everything, then I discovered one of the reasons she wanted to share. "Would you do the driving until we get past Chicago?" she asked. "I've never driven in Chicago and it scares me. I'm going as far as Findlay, Ohio. Is that good for you?"

"I'll make it good for me. I live in Columbus, but if I can get off in Toledo, I have a cousin who lives there and maybe he and his wife could put me up until I can get back to Columbus. And, yes, I'd be happy to do the driving."

Chicago is ninety miles south of Milwaukee and I had driven back and forth between those two cities many times. Because Chicago was one of my largest markets, I was there often. The accounts I called on were spread all over so I knew my way around the city and their tollway systems.

Now that we were securely in possession of a car rental contract, we could proceed to the restroom, getting something to eat and making a few phone calls, though I was a bit nervous being in an airport that could be, but was not likely to be, bombed. I called Ed first, told him the plan. I wasn't sure about the Toledo arrangements because I hadn't spoken to my cousin George in whose house I hoped to stay. Ed told me he would drive to Toledo to get me, but we should be in touch again before definite plans could be made.

I called my office in New Jersey and spoke to Bob. It was confusion and chaos there. Our other two regional sales managers were stuck; one was on the West Coast in San Francisco and Roger was in Tampa, both risky areas because of the now known terrorist attacks.

"Do what you have to do to get back home. We'll talk

tomorrow," Bob said. "It's bedlam in New York, and we know people who are lost." He was panic stricken.

Once we got the car and headed for Chicago, we were so busy listening to the radio and getting details of what had actually happened in the four terrorist attacks, we didn't talk to each other. I think I asked her name, but didn't remember it. I do know that she was married and the mother of two small children, and she worked at Marathon Oil headquarters in Findlay, Ohio.

We heard on the car radio that there could be another terrorist attack planned for Los Angeles International Airport and in Chicago at the Sears Tower downtown. Based on that information, I decided not to go through downtown Chicago, which would have been the most direct route to the Indiana and Ohio Turnpikes. Instead I took the far south and west outer belts to avoid downtown and O'Hare Airport. It took hours longer, but we felt safer. We hardly passed a car on the road.

When we reached the Indiana Turnpike she took over driving. I telephoned my cousin in Toledo who welcomed me to stay the night. Cousin George, an appeals court judge, and his wife were planning to drive to Columbus the following day for a meeting. The meeting was canceled, as was most everything throughout the country, but George and his wife, Maureen, drove me to Columbus anyway. It was a warm and sunny

September day in spite of the ugly things that had happened during the past twenty-four hours.

§

Just one more month before our wedding. My condo was for sale, but with no apparent buyers. Meanwhile, I had a houseful of furniture and so did Ed. What to keep and what to give away. Ed and I couldn't agree. He was reluctant to give up anything so we hired a "rearranger." I was always eager to clear out my belongings, but some of my furniture and things were in better shape than Ed's, and I had to sell him on the idea to keep the best of the bunch, mostly my stuff.

Ed and I hired Mary Ross, a decorator and my friend, to rearrange the interior of Ed's house using a combination of his things and mine. Her job assisting Ed with what to keep and what to give away was not easy. She did it and arranged everything in Ed's house, now mine too, satisfying both of us. She did not allow the poster of Joe Namath to hang in our living room. Ed had a problem understanding why. Furthermore, a framed poster of the toothy quarterback has disappeared from our basement. Ed can't figure that out, either.

Our wedding on Saturday night October 13, 2001, was my fourth and final union. All five of our children and our eight grandchildren were present, along with my sister and Ed's brother. On Sunday morning we had a brunch for one hundred relatives and friends. Each of our children gave a champagne toast.

Mark, my son from Connecticut, told the guests, "Last week I asked my boss for Friday and Monday off because I was going to my mother's wedding in Columbus. My boss said, 'That's fine. After all, how often does your mother get married?'" The crowd laughed and Mark said, "You don't know my mother."

CHAPTER ELEVEN
2002

Life for Americans changed on September 11, 2001, particularly for the business traveler. Flying from Columbus on Tuesday mornings, returning Thursday afternoon or evening was my routine. I flew mostly on TWA, often with a plane change in St. Louis, a major TWA hub. All of the airlines offered perks to get the business. Points, double points and triple points, along with upgrades and memberships in private clubs were dangled in front of us offering free trips to everywhere.

For a yearly fee I could belong to TWA's Ambassador Club. After a few years TWA offered a lifetime membership at a discount. I accepted the offer. The membership lasted longer than the airline but then transferred to American Airlines for a couple of years when the two airlines merged. While TWA was flying, an Ambassador Club was located in practically every U.S. major city and internationally, too. New York's JFK Airport had two as did St. Louis and other major hubs.

The Ambassador Club in Columbus was like a second home to me. My good friend Sabena was manager. I telephoned her the day before a flight, the day of and while I was on the road for seat selections, upgrades, schedule changes and when I had a problem in or out of the country. So, when I needed a wheelchair after landing in Columbus from a difficult homecoming on a flight from St. Louis, Sabena was at the gate with a wheelchair along with my husband whom she had contacted when she heard I was ill.

Ed and I had been married just a few months. He took me to the airport on Tuesdays and either he picked me up Thursday evening or I took a taxi to our house, which was less than the cost of parking and a lot faster. After September 11 security around airports was tight. For a few months private cars could not stop at the terminal for more than a few minutes while passengers were dropped off. At first, security was stationed on ramps stopping all cars before they entered terminal areas to check for weapons and explosives.

In some cities like Des Moines, Wichita or Grand Rapids, private automobiles were not allowed anywhere near the terminal. At a central location, passengers were sent to the terminal by shuttle. Rental car lots on site at airports were moved off site and shuttles were used to transport passengers and luggage. It was a terrible inconvenience, but we were a panicked nation.

So, during a cold, dark and snowy week in mid-January I was in Grand Rapids, Michigan, feeling awful. I couldn't keep food down and couldn't eat. I didn't have a fever, but the stomach pain was excruciating. Twenty-four hours later the pain had moved from the front to the back of my body and I needed to get home. Sabena was able to secure a first class upgrade quickly, but I had to change planes in St. Louis. She and Ed met me when I was first to exit the plane in Columbus. Ed had the car in valet parking warming to take me to the emergency room at OSU Medical Center.

By the time I was admitted to the ER and safely in a bed, I was in a fetal position doubled over from pain. A team of doctors examined me and sent for the on-call gastroenterologist who ordered immediate tests before consulting with Ed and me. He seemed seriously concerned. What was going through my head was that this had to have something to do with my heart, but what? During the last few months I had been diagnosed with acid reflux and was taking an over-the-counter medication for it, but on my own, I discovered that if I stayed away from certain foods and didn't overeat, I had less discomfort. This pain was nothing like I had ever had, and I have a high tolerance to pain. Not now.

"I've ordered a round of tests but your symptoms appear to be those of acute pancreatitis," the doctor said.

That's all I had to hear. I was only familiar with diseases of the pancreas having to do with pancreatic cancer, and those whom I had known with pancreatic cancer had died quickly not responding to drugs or treatment.

"Oh, Ed," I sobbed. "I'm so sorry. This is not fair to you after losing Barbara then Pat. I don't want to put you through nursing another sick wife."

Ed, being the trooper he is, appeared calm and confident and wouldn't let me feel sorry for myself. "You're going to get through this. You're strong, I'm strong and we'll beat this."

The ER unit was busy with nurses, doctors and other staff coming in to take blood, insert the IV, offer pain meds and ask a million questions. OSU was in process of going totally electronic with patient records and information, but this didn't reduce the number of questions they asked over and over as though they didn't have my records or lists of meds. When I answered one of their questions, I asked one of my own about the diagnosis. It boiled down to this: Acute pancreatitis could be fatal. It could be caused by gallstones, alcohol, medications or a list of other complaints, even genetics. All of this was covered in a multitude of questions over and over. Did I drink? How much? How often? I was never a drinker, especially because I had had hepatitis as a teenager. After I met Ed a big part of our social life, with friends and each other, was dinner in a restaurant every night. We didn't eat junk or fast food, but we ate in upscale restaurants where the food was fresh, healthy and not inexpensive. We did, however, have a drink with dinner every night. Mine was a glass of red wine, always just one glass. I liked it.

"Mrs. Ungar," the doctor said. "We have a room for you upstairs in the main hospital where you will undergo a series of tests and treatment for acute pancreatitis."

"For how long?" I asked.

"Possibly as long as a week, until you are clear. Right now you're in atrial fibrillation and your body is under stress from the pancreatitis. We'll start you on meds and nutrition will come from an IV. You are not to eat or drink anything except for ice chips, and those only in moderation. I don't want you to get out of bed. Do you have a preference for pain medication?"

I remembered that when I was in the ICU after hip replacement surgery when my heart stopped and I was scheduled for a pacemaker, I took a strong pain medication that made me groggy, but for the next few days nothing was expected of me, so why not be groggy? "I took something after another surgery a few years ago that seemed to be effective without much in the way of side effects. It was called Alotta, or something like that."

"Dilaudid," he said.

It did work and I began to time its use and how long it took to become effective after it was added to the IV in my arm. Not long. It numbed the pain but after a few days, when the pain began to subside, I wondered why some people loved the way pain killers made them feel. For me, I felt I was not totally alive, unable to make decisions. Maybe others didn't want to be bothered, and pain killers gave them an out. I loved feeling high on life with boundless energy. Dilaudid did the opposite.

The tests confirmed that I had acute pancreatitis. The doctors could only speculate as to why. One gastroenterologist said that small gallstones could have caused the acute attack, though it was unlikely. Another time when he was on rounds he told me that the amiodarone might have been the culprit. That prompted me to contact Dr. Caldwell in another part of the hospital to investigate accusations against a drug that kept my heart in rhythm ninety percent of the time for the last fifteen years. I shook with fear at the thought of not having that drug after I had tried ten other anti-arrhythmias that didn't work at all. What would happen without amiodarone? Would I be in atrial fib all of the time? Besides being a candidate for stroke, I would be exhausted, unable to work, to travel or exercise. I was familiar with that complication and I wanted no part of it.

CHAPTER TWELVE
2002

"What do you mean when you say that a small study was done on amiodarone?" I asked.

I was focused on the gastroenterologist's opinion that amiodarone, the anti-arrhythmia drug that I had been taking for fifteen years, could be the reason for my current predicament and the cause of acute pancreatitis. I had telephoned the clinic cardiologist, Dr. Patricia Caldwell, from my hospital bed and left more than one message. Normally clinic physicians did not treat or consult with in-patients while they were confined, but I needed to talk to her because I was scared and confused.

She explained that the study involved around 400 people and that two of those had developed acute pancreatitis.

"That's a pretty low number," I said. "Frankly, Dr. Caldwell, I can't see trading one risk for another. I think that I'd prefer to stay on amiodarone while we look for another solution to eliminating A-Fib altogether, and aim for looking into that new heart ablation procedure."

"Come and see me, Mrs. Ungar, and I'll let you know what I find out." After twenty years as her patient, she still never called me by my first name, but she had made a smooth transition from Mrs. Linver to Mrs. Ungar when I married Ed.

At a follow-up appointment with the gastroenterologist, he suggested that the tiny gallstones were the culprits and that if I decided to have the gall bladder removed, it could be done by laparoscopic surgery, an outpatient procedure that is minimally invasive. In my case, however, I would require one night in the hospital for observation because I was on warfarin. There was always the chance that once the surgeon entered the area, he might decide that the problem was more complex and that major surgery and cutting would be necessary to remove the gall bladder.

In my mind the explanation of minimally invasive surgery was easy to visualize: The surgeon goes into the navel with video equipment and small surgical instruments and sucks out the gall bladder, which is the size of a small slightly inflated balloon. A tiny incision is made and when it is all over the only evidence is the black thread from one or two stitches.

The day of surgery, while I was waiting to go into the operating room, a familiar young man stood next to my gurney smiling. He introduced himself as the doctor in charge of anesthetic.

"We've met before," he said. "Though you may not remember, I administered anesthetic when you had the robotic heart bypass not long ago. Dr. Wolf did that surgery."

"Oh yes," I said, trying to sound like I remembered him.

We talked, or rather he did mostly, and explained that the O.R. was backed up and it wouldn't be much longer. I had been given a shot to relax before surgery, but I still had questions and the young man who would eventually put me to sleep was in a talkative mood. He spoke about modern surgical technology and how, in today's world, a doctor didn't have to be in the same hospital as the patient, or even the same city to do surgery. It was done with a telescopic rod lens, a video camera, a digital laparoscope and a fiber optic cable system. Not sure that what he said is what I heard, my drooping eyelids were witness to less than what I thought. I may have missed a few things while dozing off, but two things I do remember: The first transatlantic laparoscopic surgery was removing a gall bladder. The other was an answer to my question about how a doctor learns that kind of eye/hand coordination using a video camera and surgical instruments on an image.

"Why, Mrs. Ungar, our generation grew up from an early age on video games. We learned eye/hand coordination from Game Boy and Nintendo."

The next thing I knew I was in my hospital room and the laparoscopic surgery was over.

CHAPTER THIRTEEN

2002

In early February 2002, Ed turned sixty-six years old. It didn't occur to me that I would be sixty-five in August. Retirement had not been part of my plan or Ed's. My boss, Bob, was not far from eighty and stepping down was not in his future either. Bob, owner and CEO of GFA Brands, Inc., creator of Smart Balance brand, had just merged his business with his son Peter, CEO of Silver Palate, a company with a line of gourmet chutneys, salad dressings and sauces in pretty packaging. The merger involved me inasmuch as my sales calls on the grocery trade all over the Midwest would now include selling some of the Silver Palate items too. I liked Peter and adored his high-end items, but wondered what this father-son combination meant.

Travel was difficult. The Transportation Security Administration (TSA) agency, a department of Homeland Security, was established not long after the terrorist attacks of September 11, 2001. Airline passengers were under a high level of scrutiny. Travelers had to put all hand and carry-on luggage, purses and coats on conveyer belts to go through sensitive machinery to detect anything that might resemble a weapon. Corkscrews, nail files, nail clippers, pocket knives and scissors were confiscated. Would-be-terrorists were discovered trying to make bombs in airline lavatories from flammable liquids they had brought on board. One terrorist tried to light a bomb in the lining of his shoe.

At some airports going through initial security was not enough. TSA also began checking passengers just outside the entrance to the Jetway. Profiling passengers who looked like they might be terrorists was prohibited, so the second check had to be at random. I went through security three or four times a week and half of the time I was one of the randomly checked passengers, which meant an electrical coil wand was to be used over my body, briefcase and purse.

A sign at the security entrance announced that passengers with pacemakers should not go through equipment but be checked by a TSA agent. I knew that security stations were OK for me, but the wand was not. It had something to do with the electrical interference caused by the security coil. Usually I didn't tell the TSA about my pacemaker, but the gate checks were different. No wand meant that I had to have a pat-down by the probing hands of a TSA agent.

Friends and clients asked me how long I was going to keep on traveling every week. "Until I can no longer lift my carry-on luggage into the overhead compartment," I said. That time was coming sooner rather than later.

My atrial fibrillation occurred more often and lasted longer. Maybe I noticed it more because it was harsher and sometimes woke me out of a sound sleep. Meager energy left me with labored breathing. My four mile walks outside and on the treadmill could only take place on days I felt good, never when I was in A-Fib. When I had a good week, I could do the four miles in an hour and accomplished fifteen to twenty miles weekly. I began to see that walking was not enough exercise. I needed upper body workouts too.

I never stayed home from work or travel when I was in A-Fib, but it was difficult getting up at five in the morning for a seven-thirty flight, parking my car, taking the shuttle, carrying luggage and going through security—sometimes twice. When I arrived at my destination, retrieving luggage, renting a car, finding that parked car and getting to the food broker's office in time for a meeting was exhausting, especially in snow, ice or rain.

Because I had been doing this routine for so many years, I was familiar with most Midwestern cities. Finding my way around Chicago, Detroit, Des Moines, Omaha, Minneapolis and St. Louis was easy, but in A-Fib, just getting into a car was an effort.

I traveled so much that I was often confused about where I was at any given time. Once, on a plane, I had a conversation about restaurants with a seat mate.

"Do you know a good restaurant in downtown Chicago?" he asked.

"There are a lot of good restaurants in Chicago," I replied. "One of my favorites is downtown between Jefferson and Michigan Ave. on East Congress. It's the London Chop House. It's fabulous and you may even see some celebrities. Ask the concierge at your hotel for directions."

He wrote my suggestion on a napkin and put it in his pocket. Later that day I realized that the London Chop House is in Detroit.

§

Ed had remodeled part of the basement in the house we shared. We now had a small but nicely furnished workout room with treadmill, mats, weights, exercise ball, bench, Bosu and stretchy bands. Ed was disciplined and did an hour or more workout three or four times a week. I tried to work out with him one weekend and couldn't do even one pushup, not one.

"What if I became disabled and had to be in a wheelchair?" I asked. "I wouldn't be able to push myself up and out."

"Retire," he said.

Another problem that I encountered was working not only at my age, but in an age of technology. My computer skills were adequate but not easy, nor did I like coming back to my hotel room in the evening having to hook up my laptop, do email, prepare the next day's agenda, write memos and reply to requests from other markets. Sometimes it took hours, mainly because the computer was difficult for me to navigate. I preferred to communicate by phone or in person. I couldn't have prepared a PowerPoint presentation under any circumstances, and that was what the industry needed. Besides, lugging around another piece of equipment from airport to airport, putting it in a now bigger briefcase and taking it out at airport security was a hassle.

I'm a sales person and I'm good at it. Face-to-face and without a college degree, I can sell just about anything. So, as long as the world is full of things to sell, I can make a living. Indeed I made a nice living for myself. For Bob, my boss, I was instrumental in building his little family-owned company into an empire. He offered this praise when he wanted to be a mensch…or when he wanted something from me. Was he getting ready to sell the Smart Balance line? Should I wait to retire to see if my phantom shares of stock in the company would be worth anything now or a year from now?

Phantom stock is not just an expression. It is real stock regulated by the rules of ERISA (the Employee Retirement Income and Security Act of 1974), a federal law that governs retirement plans. Sometimes it is tied to other employee ownership plans such as ESOP or 401-K, stock option or employee stock purchase plans. I believe that Bob wanted to share the economic value of equity, but not the equity itself. So, phantom stock is what we had. Each year our handful of employees received a report showing us how many shares we each had and an approximate value at that time. The value went up some years, and down in others.

Regardless of when I would decide to retire, my pre-determined shares would be valued at whatever equity Bob deemed applicable. Naturally, the shares would be of greater value if the company or part of the company was sold.

I decided to be open and discuss it with him. At age sixty-five I could collect full social security benefits. Some retirees took part of their benefits at age sixty-two, but I didn't do that. Now, however, the laws around this issue were changing. When a retiree born before the end of 1937 became sixty-five, the full monthly amount would be available. Retirees born after 1937 would have to consult a progressive timetable as to when they could collect at a slightly later date than prior eligibility. People were living and working longer. All retirees, however, were eligible for Medicare as soon as they reached age sixty-five. This was not a small matter.

I had had fifty years of working and contributing to Social Security. During that time I had careers, not jobs, earning wages at the top of my pay scale "for women." The 1950s and 1960s were historical times for women in the work force when there was no such thing as equal pay for equal work.

Six months before my sixty-fifth birthday in August, I decided that I would retire at the beginning of 2003, twenty-six years after starting as Bob's first sales employee. At that time he had only one other person working for him, a secretary whom he had recruited from a former company. She had come with him when he started this business and they worked out of his home until just a few months before I was hired.

I loved my job from the beginning but I did have problems with Bob keeping the promises he made concerning salary, bonuses, vacations, sick time, travel and transportation. I soon learned that I had to get his commitments in writing. Bob was a charmer, the kind of guy whom everyone wanted to please. He was a marketing genius. He was humble. When he had an idea for a new product, he let us, his small staff of employees, think that we were helping to develop it, even assist in its naming.

Fourteen people made up our entire company. Four of us were the sales department managing food brokers throughout the country. I was the only female. Throughout my twenty-six years I had confrontations with Bob because I felt I was not being treated the same as the married male staff. I was single. I didn't have a family to support, and the others had spouses and children at home. We went round and round, but it got me nowhere. I quit twice.

"Bob, there's a rumor that you have plans to sell the Smart Balance part of the business. Is that true?" I decided to be direct so there could be no misunderstanding. The future of my retirement was at stake.

Typical of this clear and decisive man who at times was stuck for an answer, he replied with a stutter. The stutter gave him time to think of an answer.

"Ah...well...uh...where did you hear that?"

"It's going through the office and staff," I said.

Howie was the only one in sales who worked from the New Jersey headquarters office. He was responsible for sales in New York, New Jersey and the rest of the Northeast. We worked out of our homes. The only time we were together was for a sales meeting in the New Jersey office or some other city.

Bob was always surprised that we talked among ourselves between these meetings. Talk, we did. I heard that Bob had already entered into negotiations with a company but had turned down their first offer.

"In a few months, Bob, I'll turn sixty-five making me eligible for retirement benefits. I know how many shares of company stock I have, but I don't know what it's worth. Naturally, working until after you sell the company would be a benefit to both of us."

"I have no plans to sell the company. You can work as long as you want. You don't have to retire," he said.

Ed and I discussed my possible retirement at length. We concluded that I needed to focus on myself, my health and free myself from the stress of travel, the job and my boss. I announced to Bob in writing and in one of our daily phone conversations that I would be retiring and that my last day of work would be Friday, January 3, 2003.

So began the last five months of employment with a family of people that I had been with longer than I had been married to any one of my four husbands or the combination of years to all of them. I had only been married to Ed for two years and knew that this time it was for real.

The last six months were full and productive for me and for the company. Bob hired a replacement and I traveled and trained him best as I could. My farewell tour of the territory and all of the people I had dealt with was gratifying. I had built and maintained a part of the food industry that would last for years after my departure. I ignored the bouts of A-Fib and hid them from those in my presence until I could find a place to lie down and rest quietly. Bob gave a celebratory dinner for me in New Jersey. He was very complimentary and told me, as he had many times before, that I was family.

A few weeks after I formally retired, I received the five figure sales bonus earned from my sales quota the prior year. Three months after that I received the check for my phantom stock, a decent amount in the low six figures.

Not long after that, Bob sold the company. Each of my fellow salesmen got $1.4 million, $1.2 million more than I had received.

CHAPTER FOURTEEN
2003-2004

I worked my whole adult life for pay. When I was in Europe, I was an au pair. When my own children were babies and I stayed home to take care of them, I also taught ballet two days per week on an army base where my husband was stationed. At age fifteen, in 1953, I had my first real job as a car-hop, serving people who drove to the restaurant, ordered a meal, and ate in their car. My job consisted of delivering a menu, attaching a tray to their roll-down window, taking the food order, bringing it to the car window and collecting money. No tipping. It was the hardest job I ever had. That was fifty years before the first day of my retirement in 2003.

Unlike many retirees, I had no plans and no other job on

the horizon, not even a hobby. I played bridge with a regular foursome on Monday nights when I wasn't traveling. Job travel usually began Tuesday mornings. I loved museums, theatre and movies, but that was not something I did on a regular basis. Certainly, I was not planning to spend much time in the kitchen. Ed and I eat most of our meals out, and the restaurant life is an enjoyable part of our socializing. I did, however, walk four miles almost every day, and that exercise would continue no matter what.

So, on day three of retirement after recalling prior discussions between Ed and me that involved improving my golf game and gaining upper body strength, I decided to check out fitness facilities. Ed went with me to sign up for a membership at the one I liked best. He could go as a guest several times each month, but he had made our basement into a comfortable exercise room for himself.

Before committing long term to the new facility, I made sure that their refund policy made it easy to change my mind. I had signed up for gyms in the past, going only two or three times and paying for months afterwards. What a waste. This fitness center anchored an upscale indoor-outdoor area of many acres that included shops, department stores, movie theatres and many restaurants specializing in a variety of cuisines with prices from cheap to outrageous. The area and development were beautiful. I could picture myself spending days working out and meeting friends for lunch, shopping and going to movies.

The two-story fitness palace had a lap swimming pool, a smaller pool for kids, a Jacuzzi hot tub for ten or twelve members, water fun and exercise slides and tubes, numerous treadmills, stationary bikes, stair climbers, benches, weight machines and equipment for body building that I had no idea how to use. On the ground floor were classrooms for small and large groups doing boot camps and workouts to music. The shower room for women housed large and small lockers, showers, steam rooms, saunas, mirrors, hair dryers and basic soaps, shampoos and cosmetics. Sweaty women of all sizes undressed without shame. I didn't like to parade naked in front of anyone. When I walked from locker to shower in a towel and bare feet, it made me feel old and self-conscious. Afraid of getting a foot fungus, I brought my own flip-flops and swimsuit, but now my backpack of clothes and purse was getting heavier with wet clothes. Walking two flights of steps to a parking garage that had a mandatory incline was exhausting after a workout, which consisted mostly of treadmill because I didn't know what else to do.

Dumping out wet and dry things at home from the backpack was another chore I disliked. The whole fitness center experience was unsatisfactory. The smoothie bar on the ground floor next to a shop selling overpriced workout clothes was fun until I discovered the smoothies were high in calories. What good was a workout if the calories dropped came back in the form of a sugary fruit drink?

The few times I went into the Jacuzzi made me so tired that I could hardly walk to my car, until I realized that I was in atrial fib. It didn't take much to figure out that there was a connection between hot tub and A-Fib. I stopped the Jacuzzi and asked someone in charge to show me what to do with weights and other machinery. I was afraid to sign up for group classes and boot camps. I watched some and decided that jumping-jacks and other high impact exercises were not good for my artificial hips or my heart. Did these group leaders and trainers know what they were doing? Did they have some certification in physical training?

Finally, I met John the trainer. He saw me struggling with a core weight machine. "Want some help?" he asked.

"I'm so frustrated," I said. "In this whole place I only know how to use the treadmill and the stationary bikes, and I'm not sure about all the gadgets on the bikes."

"Hasn't a personal trainer worked with you?"

"No, I didn't pay for a trainer."

"You are supposed to have a session with a trainer to show

you what to do and how to use the equipment. That's included in your membership. Let's do it now. Do you have the time?"

John MacLeod, personal trainer, gave me a thirty-minute workout on some of the machines and taught me how to use two-pound free weights and to do squats. "Practice this by getting out of your car without holding on to the seat or the door. Also, get up from a chair or the couch without holding on, and squat without a bench or seat, down and up like this." Standing with legs spread and back straight but slightly forward, the ten squats were almost impossible for me to do.

John gave me a quick verbal schedule of days and times he worked and could help me. He told me about the classes and boot camps he taught but insisted that I wasn't ready for those. He suggested I spend fifteen minutes on a stationary bike at the end of my workouts to cool down, and ten minutes on the treadmill to warm up at the beginning.

The treadmill was easy because I had been doing it for several years, but I hadn't done the bike since rehab after my heart attack. After five minutes on the bike my thighs were burning. That was strange. Why would my thighs be so sore after the years of walking outside and on the treadmill? John said it was not just different muscles, but more muscles in legs and hips were used without the impact of pressure. Two more minutes and the sweat was pouring down my back. After the cool down, I took my pulse. It was fine—steady with the pace-maker at a calm seventy beats per minute. No A-Fib.

The next day I could hardly get out of bed. Every muscle hurt from the previous day's workout. I was familiar with these aches and welcomed them, knowing I was doing something good for me. But some of the aches were in places I didn't know there were muscles—under the arms behind the armpits. Scary as it was, my chest was sore and initially I thought it might be my heart. It wasn't. As I got used to the exercises and added more to the routine, I would be conditioned and in control. As difficult as it was, after checking my morning steady pulse, I put on workout clothes and headed for my new gym, looking forward to seeing John the trainer.

His back was to me, but I recognized him immediately. He had a gray ponytail down the middle of his back. Yesterday it was braided. His forehead was deep as the result of some balding, not unusual for a man in his mid-forties. He wore glasses and had a handlebar mustache, also gray. Not much taller than me, he was muscular but stocky. I liked him because he had been kind and caring and he reminded me of friends I had made in the sixties and seventies, hippies, most of whom were artists. Later I discovered that John, too, was an artist working mostly with leather.

John trained me three days each week, but he couldn't

stay the whole hour with me because I wasn't paying the fitness center for a personal trainer. One day we'd work on upper body equipment and weights, the next legs—squats, sit-ups on a bench, lunges and a lot of work on balance. Aging affects balance so we worked on front, back and side lunges and on a half-ball called a Bosu. Standing on one leg for ten seconds wasn't easy, but John said to either practice that one with him nearby or next to something to hold on to. Working on the core or mid-body is important. Some core exercises can't be felt in the muscle until the next day. Crunches on a large exercise ball with arms extended or with a four-pound ball going from side to side are good core exercises. Then we worked on calf muscles with toe lifts, wall sittings, scissor and flutter kicks—all good for the core. Every day started and ended with five to ten minutes on the treadmill or bicycle. We did different exercises each day. It was never boring. On the days I was in A-Fib, I contacted John to tell him that I wouldn't be working out.

Sometimes I could exercise after the atrial fib left me and I went back into a normal rhythm, but as time went on, I was too tired after a bout of A-Fib. I worked my retirement free time around the exercise, not the other way around. One day John told me he would be leaving this fitness facility and going to another that was much smaller and only for fitness without a pool, smoothie bar or retail store. That sounded perfect for me, because I still didn't like the vastness of this place—the twenty-minute drive, the parking garage and the walk to and from. I didn't feel comfortable in the locker room and showers or even the pool, which I felt that I had to use because I was paying for it. John said it would be a few months before he made the move.

I asked John if he could train me at my home. Though we didn't have the electrical equipment in our lower level workout room, we had a Bosu, treadmill, bench, bands, an exercise ball, mats for floor exercises and a variety of free weights. If arrangements could be made immediately, I would be able to get a fair refund from the fitness center. It worked out. We agreed that three days each week he would come to the house early enough to train Ed for an hour, then me. If I was in A-Fib, he would train only Ed.

The months John trained Ed and me at home were good for both of us. Ed learned a variety of new exercises and how to do them correctly. That's one of the important values of having a certified personal trainer: learning to do the exercises correctly. Otherwise, one can get hurt and the injury could be permanent. Ed has more discipline than I. His schedule was three times a week, and he got that in no matter what. I was pretty good about getting up and ready for John on schedule, but I discovered that the most difficult part of exercise was the fifteen minutes before I started, thinking of every reason why I shouldn't be doing this. Did my back hurt? Was I getting a cold? Was it too hot? Was I too tired? Rarely did anything except atrial fib keep me from doing my workout.

Months later John announced that he would be training at the new small facility up the road from us. Ed decided to have him come to the house once a week for a little while longer. I went to the new place and loved it. Easy and fast from my garage to a parking space at the front door of the new gym. I came in workout clothes and wore the same clothes home. After a quick stop at the Starbucks on the way home, I made a beeline for the shower and turned on water as hot as I could stand it. No backpack, wet clothes or flip-flops.

The exercise habit had begun. It would be with me for the rest of my life…a self-fulfilling promise I plan to keep.

CHAPTER FIFTEEN
2005-2006

A 2005 headline in the *Columbus Dispatch* newspaper announced, "Doctors help jump-start OSU heart practice." The article revealed the move of five top electrophysiologists from Riverside Methodist Hospital to The Ohio State University's new Ross Heart Hospital, now almost finished on the medical campus of the university. The article mentioned the investment by the university in the most up-to-date equipment, and that the electrophysiologists would be able to devote considerable time to research. I referred to them as "the fab five."

Meanwhile, my friend Dave Ross had recently had a defibrillator implant at Riverside Hospital. I called Mary, his wife, to find out more.

"Did you read where OSU Hospital just hired five electro-physiologists from Riverside Hospital?" I asked Mary.

"Yes. Isn't that great? John Hummel is one of them. I'm sure you heard me talk about him. He operated on Dave and saved his life. What an opportunity for OSU Hospital and these five doctors. And, for you too."

Mary was the decorator who had done work for Ed and me when we combined two houses of furniture into one. "I desperately need to see a doctor, an electrophysiologist, who can do a heart ablation. That's the only way I'll get rid of A-Fib. The meds are getting less and less effective."

"Well, Rosalie, try to get Hummel to do it. He's an electro-physiologist and he's wonderful."

Shortly thereafter I had my regularly scheduled appointment with Dr. Caldwell. We had a lot to talk about: the new staff of electrophysiologists coming to OSU and the heart ablation now widely known and accepted as a solution to atrial fibrillation. Finally, we discussed her own retirement agenda.

"I don't want to wait until the new doctors are in place and the Ross Heart Hospital is finished," I said. "I just read in *U.S. News & World Report* that the Cleveland Clinic has a good success rate with heart ablation procedures eliminating A-Fib. I read that the head of that department is a Doctor Andrea Natale. I want to see him, Dr. Caldwell."

"Mrs. Ungar, we have a fine clinical electrophysiologist here doing procedures for atrial fibrillation. I suggest that you see him first before going to Cleveland Clinic. Besides, the new electrophysiologists coming over from Riverside Methodist will be here much sooner than you may have expected."

"Who is he, the doctor doing ablations here? When can I see him?"

I was being abrupt. I knew it showed disrespect on my part, and my friend and doctor for over twenty years didn't deserve that. Maybe I was feeling abandoned because Dr. Caldwell announced her retirement just when I needed her support the most. I didn't feel good most of the time…maybe I had one or two good days each week. The rest of the time I was tired, short of breath and scared, especially when I felt my pulse. I was scared even in regular rhythm. My apprehension before I felt the inside of my wrist was a crapshoot. It exhausted me. I was afraid that my heartbeats would be so fast that I'd be unable to get an accurate count. I feared the waiting while there was a silent gap and the pacemaker took over to get my heart going. I felt only half alive.

"Dr. David Hart is one of our brightest physicians in Cardiovascular Medicine. He practices at The OSU Medical facility in Circleville. I'll make an appointment for you before you leave here today."

Dr. Hart was located in a satellite office in downtown Circleville, a small town south of Columbus. Ed and I made the twenty-five mile trip on one of the two days weekly that the doctor saw patients. On other days the office was used for medical specialties unrelated to the heart, more specifically, unrelated to electrophysiology. The rest of the week he was at the main hospital campus in Columbus. The Circleville office didn't appear medical at all. It was a suite in a small building across the street from a dress shop, Christopher's Boutique, where I had long ago spent time and money. Around the corner was a medium-priced fish restaurant we had enjoyed with friends.

"What is your success rate in ending atrial fib with your patients?" I asked. Dr. Hart was a large fitful man with a big personality. I guessed him to be in his forties. His list of credentials was extensive. He had a background starting in Nigeria, then England, New York and finally Columbus.

"We have better than a ninety percent success rate for this procedure. It's not surgery in as much that cutting and incisions are not part of the process. We ablate the electrical pathways in the atrium that are causing abnormal heart rhythms."

I was lost in his explanations but encouraged by his success rate and my desire to do what I had to in order to feel good again. I didn't know what the word ablation meant. The Merriam-Webster online dictionary describes the verb ablate,

"To remove or destroy especially by cutting, ablating or evaporating. Intransitive verb. To become ablated; vaporize."

Google showed what seemed like a zillion other explanations, none of which I could comprehend. Then I Googled "StopAfib.org." The paragraph under *What Causes Atrial Fibrillation* read:

> *Where does atrial fibrillation come from and what causes it?*
>
> *We know that the erratic electrical impulses that cause atrial fibrillation often originate in the pulmonary veins, at least in most paroxysmal (intermittent) atrial fibrillation, and that the impulses that cause persistent and longstanding persistent atrial fibrillation are believed to come from other areas as well, but what actually causes afib? Though researchers are investigating the cause of atrial fibrillation, as of now it is largely unknown except that some recent studies have shown a genetic component as afib often runs in families.*

Well, that was a lot of nothing as far as I was concerned. I was skeptical about all explanations of A-Fib. The symptoms were terrible. But I needed to cure my disease and evidently there was a cure available. I had to find out more and make a decision.

Now I officially had two electrophysiologists: Dr. David Hart offering to proceed with an ablation, and Dr. Charles Love, in charge of my pacemaker. With heart specialists named Hart and Love, I couldn't go wrong. But I still had to investigate other options, mainly Dr. Natale at Cleveland Clinic.

"How long will the battery last on this pacemaker?" I asked Dr. Love during my next routine check.

"You have about two more years on it, maybe a little more."

Thinking about the timeline for surgical procedures, would the ablation interfere with the pacemaker action? Could they both be done at the same time? I couldn't stand two more years of A-Fib misery.

"Do you just change the battery in this one? Is it surgery or an under-the-skin procedure like when this pacemaker was implanted?"

I was hooked up with wires attached to strategic parts of my body while information strips of paper exited a computer. Dr. Love explained the next pacemaker installation. "We don't change the battery. We change the whole device. So much progress has taken place in the last five years that we install the latest equipment available. We will, however, use the same wires that are in place now and attach them to a new upgraded pacemaker… That is after we make sure there are no wire defects."

"How many pacemakers can a patient have during one's lifetime?" I asked.

"There's no limit…as many as you need. I had a patient who had eight different pacemakers."

Dr. Love gave me one of the strips from the computer with details of my pacemaker and the statistics to carry around in my wallet. I placed it next to the list of current medications. "It's important," he said, "in case of illness or accident."

§

Two weeks later, before my next appointment with Dr. Caldwell, Ed asked what I thought of Dr. Hart and would I consider having him perform the ablation.

"I don't know," I said. "I like him, but the physical location of the clinic in an office building in downtown Circleville turned me off. It seems unprofessional to be making a life decision concerning my heart at a temporary office where there's an aquarium in the examining room. It's so unmedical. I think I want to see Dr. Natale at the Cleveland Clinic before I make a decision."

It wasn't easy getting an appointment with Dr. Andrea Natale. His popularity had soared as a result of the media attention A-Fib was getting. Heart ablation news and successes pointed directly to the Cleveland Clinic. Finally, I received the appointment with instructions to bring recent medical records pertaining to my cardiac condition including catheterizations, echocardiogram and x-ray films. The schedule of appointments was to begin at eleven thirty in the morning for tests, followed by an echocardiogram at two forty and the consultation with Dr. Natale at four o'clock. Essentially, they just glanced at the information I brought with me. They took their own tests, except for the catheterization.

Dr. Caldwell met with me for the last time when she gave me the records I requested for the Dr. Natale appointment. She told me she was retiring in a few months, at the end of the year. The new Ross Heart Hospital was complete, for now. Another few floors would begin construction immediately. The new electrophysiologists from Riverside Hospital were already on campus accepting patients.

Everything was happening so fast. So fast that I hardly had time to mourn the academic departure of my friend and trusted physician. At my last visit with her, she went over the biographies of the new "fab five" doctors and suggested the one she thought would best fit my problems, unless I had a different choice. I did.

"Well, Dr. Caldwell, the one whose work I know best from a former patient, and whose bio I've studied, is Dr. John Hummel. If I am a candidate for the heart ablation and I have it done here at the Ross, I'd like to have Dr. Hummel do it and for him to take care of my atrial fibrillation problems."

Non-committedly, she said she would put in my request.

The two-and-a-half-hour drive to Cleveland was quiet. Ed and I were deep in thought about what could happen. "If I do have the ablation in Cleveland," I said, "it'll be difficult to schlep up here from Columbus for follow-up appointments, and what if I have an emergency following the procedure after returning home?" Ed nodded. Was that a nod of agreement, or was he just acknowledging my comment? Nevertheless, I was in charge of making my own decisions about my body. I'd always felt that way and, so far, it had worked out.

The Cleveland Clinic was a city in itself and would soon expand. Fortunately, the information regarding my schedule of appointments included precise directions of where to park and where to go for each procedure, along with directions for which entry door, elevator, skyway, floor and desk to encounter. Phone numbers for each desk were documented in case we got lost or if we would be held up at one desk making us late for another appointment. I never saw such organized instructions.

The entire afternoon went smoothly and on time. Promptly at four o'clock we were seated in Dr. Natale's office with an assistant taking a full history of my heart problems and answering my preliminary questions.

Just as we finished, Dr. Natale came in. He was bigger than life. He had an air of confidence and unblemished arrogance that gave me the impression he knew what he was doing. This was confirmed when he started to talk. He explained the ablation procedure with a series of charts and diagrams of the heart, much of which I had seen and studied before. He talked about the negatives—strokes, drugs, blood thinners and follow-up problems, but when I asked about genetics, he held back with sighs that little was known about genetics in relation to atrial fibrillation.

He agreed that I was a candidate for the procedure. But they were backed up currently, even though they could do several heart ablations each day. He told me that I would be given a date for the procedure before I left the clinic.

"Dr. Natale, what is your rate of success?"

Emphatically, he said, "Ninety-five percent. This is a procedure that can be done over and over. If it doesn't work the first time, we will do it again, essentially until it is successful." I was satisfied with that answer.

"You're taking amiodarone for arrhythmia now. It's working less and less for you and that will get worse. However, in order to perform the ablation, your body must be free of amiodarone completely. That drug is a slow exit from your system. We cannot do the ablation with any amiodarone still active."

"How long will it take to get it out?" I asked.

"Six months. I can replace it with another drug that doesn't have the same lasting length in the bloodstream, but you'll have to try it for three days as an in-patient. I see that you live in Columbus. You can do the drug trial there instead of coming here to Cleveland."

"What's the drug?" I asked.

"The brand name is Tikosyn. The generic term for it is dofetilide. It relaxes an overactive heart and improves the efficiency of the heart's pumping action."

I was prepared to try anything in my desperation to get rid of atrial fibrillation, but I knew, in my heart, that it wouldn't work. I had tried so many anti-arrhythmia drugs ending in "ide" and none of them had worked.

Prescription in hand, Ed and I left the Cleveland Clinic with both hope and despair. Hope because we now knew that there was a possible cure for my affliction. Despair because of the wait and distance I would have to endure to experience it.

I called Dr. Caldwell and reported the results from the appointment with Dr. Natale. Dr. Caldwell arranged for me to see Dr. Love who would be in charge of the Tikosyn drug trial at the Ross Heart Hospital.

The drug kept me out of A-Fib for the first two boring days. According to doctors, the amiodarone was still in my system and probably of some use in keeping me out of A-Fib. Once or twice a day Dr. Love would come by with five or six students who seemed to love and respect him. He was smart and funny.

On the second day he said that my potassium levels were low. I took that to mean that the new drug was affecting potassium for which I already took medication. He asked his students what they would suggest. Either one of the students, or maybe it was I, spoke up, "Eat bananas."

Dr. Love chuckled and said, "It would take a banana longer than the length of this room to make a significant difference in the potassium level. We'll try adjusting the drug dosage and the potassium she now takes."

On the morning of the fourth day I was discharged from the hospital and filled the prescription to take home. That night I went into atrial fibrillation and it lasted more than twelve hours. I went to sleep with the irregular heartbeat and woke up with the same jumpy rhythm. That's the scariest part of all. Going to bed at night in A-Fib, my last thoughts before closing my eyes were, would I wake up with it in the morning? Or, would I wake up at all?

Ed and I had a serious talk about where to have the ablation done. The Cleveland Clinic was not an option. I had a perfectly good hospital and staff of doctors just a few miles away. I phoned Dr. Caldwell and asked her if she could make an appointment for me with Dr. Hummel. We had not yet met him.

Dr. Hummel entered the examining room with a strong and deliberate pace, full of confidence. A slender man in his mid-forties, showing no gray in his full head of brown hair, he smiled as he introduced himself. Sitting at the computer stationed in the room, he looked at my chart and further checked the notes and printouts he had in his hands. OSU Medical Center is fully computerized with patient information available to every doctor the patient has seen whether in cardiology or endocrinology or some other specialty.

I don't know how much time he usually allowed for each patient consultation, but Dr. Hummel talked to Ed and me like we were the only patients he had, not hurrying us at all. He explained atrial fibrillation, what caused it and how the ablation works. He, like Dr. Hart and Dr. Natale, said that the cure rate was in the plus ninety percent range. The ablation, as I had discovered, is not surgery and the rate of success is high. Dr. Hummel repeated that it could be done again, if not successful the first time.

Ed and I came away from that appointment feeling confident in Dr. Hummel and what the ablation could do for me. He confirmed that I was not a candidate for it until the amiodarone would be out of my system, months away. It was also verified that the dofetilide (the Tikosyn) didn't work for me.

An appointment was made for the ablation to be performed at the Ross the following January. I would not be taking an anti-arrhythmia drug during the wait. My only protection against a stroke would be the blood thinner warfarin. It was not yet known how much of the time I would be in atrial fibrillation or how I would feel during the five months of waiting. Sadly, I would soon find that out.

CHAPTER SIXTEEN
2007

John, my personal trainer, was moving to Arizona. He offered to continue training through Skype, but I didn't think I had the discipline to do a hands-on workout using a visual device. Sorry to lose him, I needed the social contact especially now while I waited for my heart ablation procedure.

More fitness centers were opening. Friends offered to introduce me to their trainers. It had been almost four years since I started training with John in 2003. Now the exercise was essential.

I interviewed some trainers but chose to work with the one at our golf club. The small fitness center across the parking lot from the club house and bag drop was tightly fitted with three treadmills, an elliptical machine, weights, benches, pulleys, bands, cables, medicine balls, exercise balls of various sizes, ropes and stationary bicycles, different from those I had previously used. These were spinning bikes. Yikes. I had taken a spinning class at Canyon Ranch Spa in Arizona where my sister Joan had taken me for my sixtieth birthday. I could only stay on the bike for a few minutes. Moves were different on the fast peddling stationary without a comfortable seat.

The new personal trainer, Paul Holmes, had two assistants. This was not one-on-one training but circuits of four to eight people doing two or more different sets of exercises and a few on cardio machines. The room was crowded, and we had to make every inch of space count.

I recognized Paul's South African accent as soon as I met him. He's a salesman and has qualities I admire most in people. His sincerity and eagerness to please and be helpful made me want to trust him. I'm glad that I did. Paul was born in Lebanon, adopted by South African missionaries, and grew up in Cape Town. I got to know him, his wife, Betsy, their two small children, and I also met Paul's dad from Cape Town and Paul's sister while she visited the U.S. from Lebanon.

It was important that Paul know and understand my health problems and that he approve of training me with my limitations. I was hoping, of course, that some of the limitations would be temporary and that after the heart ablation the atrial fibrillation would go away. I explained that I had two artificial hips and that it wouldn't be long before I turned seventy. Training me would either be a challenge or an opportunity. He smiled and said, "I will work with you. When can you start?"

"Now," I said, thankful that I was wearing clothes and shoes suitable for this first session. It would show him how much I could do.

Paul Holmes is also an outstanding athlete. Not yet thirty years old, he had participated in sports worldwide by the time he came to Columbus. When I met Paul, his major interest was rugby, a popular contact team sport in Europe and Africa, less popular in the United States. While he was building a business as a personal trainer, he was also organizing a local rugby team to compete with others in cities throughout the United States. Paul is my height and all muscle. He is compact and looks Middle Eastern. He has a great sense of humor.

Paul liked to tell stories about when he traveled by air and went through security by himself and with his family, none of whom look Middle Eastern. Some stories were funny, some were sad, and some made us realize how difficult life could be outside the mold.

We discussed cost and schedule. For a set price payable up front, I could come and go as many times per week as I wanted over a period of five or six months. Usually, if my heart was in regular rhythm, I worked out three or four times a week. Sometimes more. Sessions were forty-five minutes. Groups were five or six people, many of us doing different exercises at the same time. We did a lot of weight training. I worked with three-pound up to ten-pound weights depending on the exercise. Stretches and curls were with heavier weights. Overheads and arm raises were with lighter ones. I learned to use the TRX, a suspension training device boosting power and core using one's own body weight holding on to miracle fiber bands suspended and anchored to the ceiling.

I was, by far, the oldest person in any of the groups working out with Paul and his assistants. Men and women were between thirty and fifty years of age—some were children in their teens and twenties, offspring of the regulars. Occasionally, a sixty-plus client appeared but didn't stay long term. Paul and his assistants watched me carefully with each workout circuit. Often they tailored exercises to my condition and age, using lighter weights and cautious of my artificial hips. I don't think the exercise threw me into A-Fib. Either I had it earlier and would cancel the session, or I'd go into it later that day.

The four years I had worked with John made a tremendous difference in my strength. On the first day with John, I couldn't do even one push-up or squat. I was now in better condition than ever, except on those days my heart rhythm acted up. On normal days I could run up a flight of steps without huffing and puffing. On A-Fib days just getting to a flight of stairs was difficult. I took one step at a time, resting at every two or three.

As the amiodarone left my system, more atrial fib entered. By November of 2006, I was in A-Fib more than fifty percent of the time. My body had little energy and strength and less as each day progressed. On days when I woke up in regular rhythm, still tired, I made my way to the gym, where Paul tailored a milder workout. It was important to generate movement, then go home and sleep.

The bedroom recliner chair became my best friend. There were days I barely left it. If Ed didn't make the bed before he went to work, it didn't get made. Annoyed at the sight of any unmade bed, I was unable to lift and carry the heavy quilt bedspread to its position. This was important to me.

§

That year I looked forward to the end of the holiday season so I could get on with fixing my heart. The ablation procedure was never fearful even when preliminary tests produced some complexities.

Tests and consultations for the upcoming January 23 ablation began the second week of the month with Dr. Hummel outlining a schedule of appointments and explanations. A week after a chemical stress test, I was scheduled for a TEE (Trans-esophageal Echocardiography) test that uses sound waves to make detailed pictures and video of the heart's muscle, chambers and blood vessels.

After the TEE, the CT (Computed Tomography) scan took place. Similar to an MRI test, both are used for imaging. Patients with pacemakers cannot usually receive an MRI but can have a CT scan. It has to do with the magnets, as I was warned when the pacemaker was inserted eight years prior.

At my final consultation with Dr. Hummel before the procedure, he told me that the tests showed images of what must be done. There were five electrical pathways that needed to be ablated. One of them, however, was close to the esophagus. He wasn't sure that he would attempt to ablate that pathway for fear of damaging that organ.

Disappointed, I asked, "What can we do?"

"There is a procedure not yet approved by the FDA (Food and Drug Administration) for that problem," Dr. Hummel said. "That doesn't help us right now, but we will go ahead with the ablation on the other pathways, and possibly go back in at a later date if we need to. Meanwhile, Christine will give you details about preparations for next Tuesday morning here at the Ross. Call us if you have questions."

Christine came into the examining room with a sheaf of papers. She went over them with me almost word for word. Finally, she handed me a prescription for the drug Lovenox, an anticoagulant injection that helps to prevent the formation of blood clots. As I understood it, this would be a replacement for warfarin a few days before the ablation. Other restrictions for this medication existed, she explained. My eyes widened in horror while she told me how it would be administered.

"Don't worry," Christine said. "Ask the pharmacist to go over the instructions with you until you are sure you understand fully. Call me if you have questions."

Everyone seemed to be eager to answer my questions, but the biggest one was: *Where can I go to hide? I don't want to do this!*

Ed went to the CVS with me. I wanted him to hear and understand the complicated instructions for injecting me in the stomach with Lovenox. He agreed to comply. The pharmacist handed us a square box containing the vials and premeasured medication contained in each injection device and a small container for the used syringes to be disposed after use.

The cost would be high because the copay was expensive—more than any of my other prescriptions had ever been. Medicare would pay for the drug, but it would use up much of my yearly allotment of insurance for prescriptions, plus the out-of-pocket copay. And, it was only January, with a whole year to go for Medicare insurance on regular meds. Surely I would be the one paying for all pills by October. Small price to pay for saving my life, I kept telling myself, especially as Ed was stabbing me in the stomach twice a day.

Five o'clock in the morning was check-in time at the hospital. It didn't matter that I was tired or that I wore no makeup after scrubbing in the shower with an antiseptic liquid soap. Toothpaste was the closest I got to nourishment.

Dr. Hummel stopped by to greet us and to tell Ed where to remain so that he could get frequent updates on my progress. The Ross was new and comfortable for waiting families, and the technology for gaining information was top notch. Ed was informed that the ablation procedure could take four hours or more.

After a snooze of undetermined length, following an injection to make me relax, the narrow gurney was wheeled into an operating room that looked like a television studio. On one side was another room dimly lit with a picture window looking out to where I was. It was a room within a room like a TV control room with several monitors elevated above director/doctor chairs on rollers. Above me in the main studio there were more monitors and a staff of nurses and doctors preparing for the ablation. They hovered around me giving instructions in hushed tones.

Assuming that the information on the monitors was taken from the CT scan and the TEE, it seemed like mapping test results would guide instruments in doing their work. I remembered that it was icy cold in the room and that the dulled brightness became like dusk.

Someone told me to sit up while large gel patches were placed against my back. I remember saying that I was so cold. Then something was stuck in my groin. I was prepared for that, after having more than one catheterization during recent years. Still, it hurt and I cried out in pain. I was half awake for a little while longer responding to instructions for simple maneuvers.

Waking up in recovery with other patients' beds around me, I saw Ed first. It was important that I lie flat. Ed told me that the procedure went well and that it took almost five hours. Dr. Hummel joined us and explained that he had ablated four of the five troubled electrical pathways and that the fifth one, close to the esophagus, might not give me any trouble.

I felt pretty good and was soon wheeled to a room where I would spend the night under watchful care. If all went well, I could go home the next day. And, I did, after blood tests, INR checking blood thinner levels, and starting warfarin again. Follow-up appointments were made. I was to remain quiet and rest at home the remainder of that day. The day after, Thursday, I was to come back to the hospital for another INR test. After that, it could be life as usual with sensible restrictions.

On Friday, three days after the ablation, I felt better than I had in weeks, months and maybe even years. I went shopping without getting tired. My cell phone rang just as I was leaving the Nordstrom parking lot. It was OSU Hospital calling to tell me that yesterday's INR blood test showed that levels were low and I needed to increase the blood thinner dose.

"How much more should I take and when?" The voice at the other end asked if I still had any Lovenox vials unused. "Yes," I said.

"Have your husband give you an injection of Lovenox this evening before bedtime. Come into the Ross blood draw on Monday for another INR check." I hung up dejected. Little did I know that I'd be back at the hospital long before Monday.

Disappointed in anticipation of having to go through another injection of the awful blood thinner, I whimpered as Ed emptied the small vial of liquid into my flesh. Sleep was fitful, waking me up in darkness to the worst pain I've ever felt. At first it was like nerve pain in my groin where a needle had gone just a few days prior. Unable to move out of bed and get to the bathroom where I could close the door and turn on a light, I felt for blood on the sheet or me. There wasn't any.

I could hardly keep from crying out. Ed awoke knowing something was wrong. I stood up. That was worse. Ed's gentle hand guided me to the recliner. He gave me two extra-strength Tylenol and covered me up with a quilt. Nothing helped. He coaxed me into trying to get some sleep until morning, when we would get in touch with the doctor.

Daylight didn't help the pain. It was Saturday and the regular staff was not on duty. An emergency room doctor returned Ed's call and told him to bring me into the ER as soon as possible. The pain had not moved from the groin. When we arrived outside the ER, an attendant was waiting and helped me into an examining room right away while Ed parked the car.

The doctor in charge examined me and could see my pain. He asked if I had a pain medication choice. I asked for Dilaudid. It did little to lessen my discomfort. Soon I was admitted as a patient on the heart floor of the main hospital. Doctors came in and out of the room. Some I knew, and some I didn't. They were all aware of the ablation I had earlier in the week. Pushed on a gurney by attendants to a variety of rooms with bulky equipment, my heart, groin and other parts of my body were tested and photographed. Blood was taken several times. I went in and out of restless sleep.

Finally, I heard hushed conversation at the bottom of my bed using the word "fistula."

So that those in the room would know I was awake and observing them, I asked, "What is a fistula?"

Trying to clear my head, I wanted to understand what was going on. Ed was in the room, another set of ears. The doctor wasn't sure it was a fistula. He said it looked like an abnormal connection between a blood vessel or vein and/or artery in the groin. Probably there was too much blood thinner and an adjustment in dosage would correct the problem in a day. I was to stay in the hospital and possibly go home on Monday, which I did.

CHAPTER SEVENTEEN
2007

I was back on warfarin. Since starting it again, I had to have an EKG and a pacemaker check and my INR had to be tested every two weeks. Now, before my first appointment with Dr. Hummel, he was checking the test results.

"No A-Fib shows up on the pacemaker since the ablation. EKG looks good. How do you feel?"

"I feel good almost every day for the first time in years. Am I cured? Can I go off the warfarin?"

"Your pacemaker has less than two years battery life left. We should look into switching it out in about a year, maybe less." He read the pacemaker printout. "It was installed in November of 1999. We aren't ready to take you off a blood thinner yet. I want to see you again in three months."

"What about the problem electrical pathway that couldn't be ablated because of its closeness to the esophagus?" I asked.

"We'll keep watching it. You aren't on an anti-arrhythmia drug, but the warfarin will keep you safe in case you go back into A-Fib."

I used my new-found energy to keep busy with everything. Going to the gym at 8:00 a.m. three, sometimes four or even five days a week was the catalyst that I thought made me feel good and full of energy. My workout partners became new friends. My muscle aches became evidence of living. My golf game improved, though I didn't much care to play with the ladies. I preferred to play with Ed on Sundays. Sometimes we played nine holes after he finished working during the week, then had dinner at our golf club. I played bridge on Monday afternoons. Wednesdays I attended Ohio Writers' Guild and began writing again after years of writing television promotional copy.

The CATCO theatre board took up a lot of time. It was enjoyable community service. Another group of friends led us to more community activities and entertainment. We traveled to see my children and grandchildren and Ed's too. My favorite short vacation was to New York for a few days to see plays and visit my kids in Connecticut. Without the fear of A-Fib, I could make plans again, which I was afraid to do before the ablation. If I wanted to have guests for dinner or a party, I could do it now. Before, if I scheduled an event and went into A-Fib, I had to cancel.

Life was good. If I had less than a perfect day and was tired, I figured it was because I was approaching seventy.

July, six months after the ablation and three months after my first follow-up, I went back to see Dr. Hummel. We followed the same procedure—a pacemaker check, then an EKG and into an examining room for a modest wait while he checked my chart.

He walked into the room without his normal upbeat stride, test results in hand. "How do you feel?" he asked.

"I feel good. Why? Is something wrong?" I asked. I had a feeling that all was not OK.

"You've been in A-Fib more than five hundred times since your last check three months ago."

"Five hundred times?" I asked incredulously. "But, I haven't felt them. How could that be? I take my pulse, but not as often as I used to. Is it the one pathway close to the esophagus? Is that causing the problem?"

"Possibly," he said.

"What do we do now? Go back and do the ablation again?"

He sat down looking defeated and checked the test results again. "Not right away. I want to try another anti-arrhythmia drug."

"Something new?" I asked.

"No. It's been around but you haven't been on it. Even if you had and it wasn't successful then, it could be now." He was trying to be positive, but finding it difficult, I thought. "You only have one electrical pathway that hasn't been ablated. You had five before the procedure. It could be that was too much for the drug's effectiveness."

"What's the drug?" I asked.

He got up from the chair and slowly started pacing the small examining room. "The drug is sotalol. It needs to be started as an in-patient. How soon can you check in?"

"How long do I need to be here?"

"Three days for continuous monitoring."

I looked at my pocket calendar noting that Ed and I were going to New York for the weekend, returning Sunday night. "I can start Monday."

With in-patient drug trials, some serious side effects could be evident within hours of the drug entering my system. Dosing would be determined as a result of tests after a day or two of surveillance. I'd lost count of how many in-patient drug trials I'd had in the past twenty years of A-Fib.

"What are some of the less serious side effects?"

He sat back down like he was taking a load off his feet.

"Oh, the usual," he said gloomily. "Headache, slow heart-beat, fatigue, weight gain."

I let this register while feeling sorry that he was feeling the setback so badly.

Trying to sound upbeat I said, "Well, if the fatigue is caused by a slow heartbeat, wouldn't my pacemaker fix that? The pacemaker keeps me at seventy beats a minute with or without meds, doesn't it? And, as a lifetime Weight Watchers member, if the medication only causes weight gain because of increased appetite, I think I can control my eating. Any other sotalol side effects that I should know?"

"We'll check creatinine levels before final dosing is decided. You should also know that some drug interactions could produce serious complications. Carry a list of your medications at all times and discuss with your pharmacists any new meds, prescription or non-prescription. Your current daily list is OK, but be aware that some antibiotics for infections could have deadly consequences."

I didn't ask, but told myself that this must be another dangerous heart drug. I guessed that they were all dangerous to different degrees, but I wanted to know everything there was to know about sotalol, even the rare side effects that are in small print at the end of a four-page printout.

"You will need to come into the pharmacy clinic for an antiarrhythmic meds check and EKG every six months," Dr. Hummel said.

He went on to say that new information was always coming out and that at the sotalol clinic, the pharmacologists would discuss changes. From years of checking blood thinner INR, and levels of other heart drugs, I knew most of the pharmacologists, and they knew me. When I first met Margie then Melissa, they were starting out at the Ross Heart Hospital. Now each had a husband and children. We had a mutual personal respect as was the case with most of the staff at the Ross.

"What are the antibiotics that have dangerous interactions with sotalol?" I asked.

One he told me about was an antibiotic I took several years ago, when I had a reaction to some bad drinking water. The drug worked and I recovered, but I wasn't taking sotalol. Another I took for occasional sinus infections until I discovered the small print on the package that said not to take with certain heart medications. Later, I read that a popular antibiotic was on the list to avoid. It wasn't deadly, just less effective if taken within four to six hours of sotalol. This started me reading all of the small print on every pill I swallowed or chewed. There were some surprises. I learned that antacids taken within two hours of many antibiotics and some other medications can reduce that prescription's effectiveness. Another drug has to be kept in its original package to keep it protected from moisture, never stored in a pill box.

My take-away from this information was to do the homework. Ask questions. Follow directions. My last question to Dr. Hummel that day before checking into the hospital for the sotalol drug trial was, "I only have one troubled electrical pathway and haven't felt the A-Fib since the other four were ablated, so what would happen if I didn't take the sotalol?"

"The risk for stroke would be greater," he said. "Atrial fib begets atrial fib."

CHAPTER EIGHTEEN
2008

Mother said that she didn't feel old until she turned seventy. That was in 1971. In 2008 I was already seventy. I felt terrific. I had none of the side effects one is supposed to acknowledge in "old age."

Many of my friends and family have been fortunate to have good health most of their lives. So, when they reach their seventies and suffer aches and pains, worn joints, poor eyesight, acid reflux and less energy, they develop negative attitudes. But complaining never helps.

I've had health issues practically all of my life. So far they've been fixable but not without effort, sacrifice and good health insurance. I don't take lightly the need for preventive maintenance.

Mother told me to take good care of my teeth. Dad told me the same. Both of my parents had problems with gums and teeth. This was before we had implants and gum scraping. Mother and Dad had false teeth. "Do whatever you have to do to keep your teeth," Mother would say. But I had never had dental insurance. I couldn't afford implants. And I didn't want false teeth. Keeping teeth and gums healthy became mandatory.

Then I read that good dental habits can prevent a lot of diseases and help keep the heart healthy. Regular dental visits became a necessity for me. I was shocked when the dentist said my gums would need surgery if I didn't start flossing every day or night. The nightly before-bed-habit of flossing, double flossing, stimulating the gums with wooden strips then rinsing with mouthwash saved me.

The get-ready-for-bed process takes thirty minutes or more. Years later I realize that my marriages might have produced more children if my husbands had not been sleeping by the time I finished flossing.

§

Dr. Hummel was pleased with the way sotalol was working to keep me out of A-Fib. I hadn't had any episodes since starting that drug. Now it was time to replace my current pacemaker.

The procedure for replacing the pacemaker would take

place in late January 2008, exactly one year after the ablation. I would stay overnight in the hospital.

In the operating room, staff asked me questions about prior heart surgeries and procedures. I went through the list starting after the initial pacemaker insertion, two heart attacks… last one in Omaha while I was giving a speech on heart-healthy foods. Then I described the robotic bypass surgery which was done early in its history.

"Who did that surgery?" Dr. Hummel asked while he checked the line-up of instruments he would soon use for my procedure.

"Dr. Wolf. Do you know him?"

"That was before I came here," Dr. Hummel said. "Randall Wolf was the first surgeon in the U.S. to perform a coronary bypass using the da Vinci robotic surgical system."

"I may have been one of the first women to have that surgery in Columbus," I said.

All of the information was in The OSU Medical Center computer and on a chart, but I was happy and awake enough to go over it now, making sure that each person was aware of why I was here.

The new pacemaker stored information and downloaded it during regularly scheduled checkups. It recorded my continuous heart rhythm, whether or not I had been in A-Fib, date of

A-Fib, time of day and how long it lasted. I carried a card in my wallet with all its information and updated the card after each device check. At airport security I still didn't reveal that I had a pacemaker, unless the agent wanted to use an electronic wand on me.

§

Before Dr. Patricia Caldwell retired, she was both my cardiologist and my electrophysiologist. Now I had Dr. Hummel, an electrophysiologist. But because of my history of two heart attacks and bypass surgery, I also needed a cardiologist. The heart attack follow-ups had nothing to do with the atrial fibrillation follow-ups. The pharmacologists had dealings with both doctors, even though all information and medications were in the online documentation.

I was given a list of cardiologists and asked if I had a preference. I looked each one up online and studied their backgrounds, certifications and awards. I also judged age, gender and smile. So I chose Dr. Subha Raman.

Because Dr. Raman has been involved with me while my heart health is on the upswing, I only see her once a year. I am currently in one of my productive decades, with relatively good health overall.

Looking back, I had made various lifestyle changes that

produced remarkable health results. Devotion to exercise is one of them. Paul the trainer continued to push me harder and mix cardio with weights and floor exercise. Pedaling while standing up on the spinning bicycle was the hardest. That was in 2008. At first I could only stand and pedal for twenty seconds. Eventually I got to forty-five seconds, then a year later to a minute, three to six times at intervals with other exercises.

My appetite decreased, whether from exercise, age or acid reflux. Slowly my weight began to drop, and I could see muscle definition in my arms and shoulders. I sat erectly now without thinking. My endocrinologist, Dr. Cataland, was also my primary care physician. I asked him about my digestive system and why certain foods gave me chest pains. Twice I had gone to the emergency room thinking I was having a heart attack because of the pains. Both times they did extensive testing, keeping me overnight once. They found no evidence of a heart problem.

"If the pain moves to the right side of your chest, it is unlikely that it's a heart problem," the doctor said. "Try over-the-counter acid reducer medication." I did. It produced some help but only when I started eliminating certain foods. Dr. Cataland sent me to a gastroenterologist who tested the length of time it took for food to leave my stomach. He had me eat oatmeal during the examination. It didn't produce any problems. Maybe if he had tried a hot dog with chili, I would have had some discomfort.

So, over the years, when digestive problems got a little worse, I reduced portion size, gave up dairy products and started to eat a Mediterranean diet with small quantities more frequently. Overeating is the culprit. But, sometimes you don't know you've overeaten until it's too late.

Dr. Cataland offered to give me another medication to try, but I declined. Once, food had been the most important object in my life. Now it wasn't. I liked it that way. And, I liked the thirty pounds I lost.

During one of my semi-annual checkups, Dr. Cataland's associate took over in the examining room. She said my recent labs showed that the amount of thyroid medication I was taking was on the high side of the median numbers. "We would like to have you take just a little less."

She was softening the issue because she knew how afraid I was to play with thyroid dosage. I had many years of trial and error finding the right thyroid medication, and it made life difficult until the correct brand and dosage were found. "Why do you think it is out of whack now?" I asked.

"Could be too much for the body weight you are now, or maybe because you are older," she said, looking at my age on the chart. "After all, you are past seventy."

"But I feel so good now."

"Yes, I understand that, but studies show that most changes take place between seventy-five and eighty-five."

I would have liked not hearing that.

CHAPTER NINETEEN

2008

Getting life back after the heart ablation was like being reborn. Valuing my time and efforts, I became more active in what interested me most, whether in community theatre, healthy eating, sports, writing and even shopping. Everything, however, centered on exercise. Paul, the personal trainer, was a constant.

Ed and I traveled in the U.S. and Europe. We took three theatre trips—two to London and one to Ireland. We went to France to see friends. A trip to visit Ed's daughter Elizabeth, who had been living for two years in Hong Kong with her husband, Jon, and their two little boys, proved to be an ordeal.

Jon worked for an American company that sent his family to Hong Kong as expats. Their sons were not yet school age, but they were enrolled in a private Chinese-Jewish preschool with other expat children from all over the world. English was spoken in the school, but the children also learned Mandarin and Hebrew. Elizabeth and her family lived comfortably in a high rise apartment building with hundreds of other expat families. They loved the captivating life and excitement of Hong Kong.

Elizabeth invited us to visit them, and in March of their second year we did. The ten-day stay included two days of travel. It's a long way from Ohio to Hong Kong and the time difference of twelve hours made for a difficult adjustment.

I told Dr. Hummel of our upcoming plans to visit family in Hong Kong, and that I was apprehensive going so far from home. Adjustments to my medications for subsequent bouts of atrial fibrillation were still new and so was my second pacemaker, installed two months before.

"What if I go into A-Fib or have some other problem?" I asked.

"You mean staying in it and feeling it for more than a few minutes?"

"That, or something else," I said. "Unlikely that I would have a stroke, right? I'm still on warfarin."

"Yes," he said, "but you have to work out timing your

medications with the twelve hour time difference. I have a colleague in Hong Kong. I've known him for several years, lectured there and gone to conferences with him in other parts of the world. He has an office mid-town in Hong Kong. I'll give you his contact information before you leave."

I didn't think I would need Dr. Hummel's contact, but I did.

§

The morning rush in Hong Kong proved to be like that in any major city, but worse because of an enormous island population in a small area faced with not enough bridges, boats and tunnels. However, their commuter train system was the best I'd ever seen, and their technology for moving people quickly remains, in my mind, better than anywhere, even now years later.

Jet lagged and weary, I was revived when we were met by Elizabeth and two active little boys, Isaac and Jack, Ed's grandsons. Elizabeth was expert in driving their right-handed Honda on the left through hilly crowded streets and curvy roads to the circular entrance of our hotel. We piled out of the small car and into the hotel lobby trying to keep up with the two and five-year-old children. They were running and laughing, playing tag among the guests. Spotting the bank of open elevators waiting to close doors, Jack and Isaac continued screaming with delight as they ran in and out of the empty cars momentarily headed up to as many as thirty floors.

While Ed and Elizabeth were in conversation at registration, I saw what was going on with the little boys. I ran after them in panic. What if an elevator door closed and none of us knew where they went? What if the two-year-old was alone in an elevator? Would he get off when it stopped? Would he stay on and not know how to get back down?

I ran after them. They ran faster and into an empty car. I threw myself between the elevator doors as they started to close. Just then Ed, Elizabeth and the bellman approached with our luggage. No one knew my desperation, especially Jack and Isaac. My vacation mood was set. All I could do was persevere.

I was mesmerized by the people milling in the streets and stores, restaurants and parks. The weather was cool and pleasant now, but soon would be hot and humid. We spent time playing with Isaac and Jack in their hilltop high rise apartment and park-like grounds.

The complex of multi-floored apartment buildings was full of young families from a variety of countries. Most were expats from Europe, Australia, South Africa, Israel, United States and Canada. English was the most common language. Next was French. I heard from my sister in Columbus that our cousin from Johannesburg was an expat living in that community. I hadn't seen cousin Ari since I visited his family in South Africa in 1978. He was a child then. I was unable to locate him in Hong Kong in 2008.

All the expat families had live-in maids. Maricel lived with and worked for Elizabeth and Jon. She was from the Philippines, as were most of the maids. Some were from Indonesia. Maricel did all the housework and laundry, cooked the meals and took care of Isaac and Jack. Ed and I were also her satisfied dinner guests.

The young expat mothers had a lifestyle not to be repeated when they returned to the U.S. It was sorority-house-social life, but with kids. While we were in Hong Kong, Elizabeth was preparing to go on a holiday to Macau with her expat girlfriends and their kids. The maids, including Maricel, were going along to take care of the children while the mothers enjoyed themselves at the shops, casino and spa.

People were everywhere. They were so tiny, especially the women. Elizabeth was small and athletic wearing a size zero to extra small, but in Hong Kong that translated to a size large. I was gargantuan in comparison.

Elizabeth took us on a shopping tour of Hong Kong. For many tourists that's all they do...shop. The most fun for me was not the shopping, but getting to the shopping. Hong Kong's half mile of outdoor escalators called Central Mid-level Escalator, is the longest escalator system in the world. It's under cover and free.

Starting at the top of the hill where Elizabeth's high rise and other buildings sit nestled on a peak, it's a twenty-minute trip to the bottom where a metro train station is a few steps from the escalators and can take passengers anywhere on the island using the Octopus Card. Once purchased, the Octopus contactless smart card can be used for most transportation and wherever there's an Octopus scanner. No need to remove the card from wallet or purse.

Taken with the number of people wearing medical masks over their noses and mouths, I recalled hearing that a flu epidemic had hit Hong Kong. I remarked to Elizabeth how peculiar this looked.

"Schools have been closed this week because of the flu," she said. "So far Isaac and Jack's school hasn't closed, but it may happen."

It did happen and the children were all taken on field trips to the zoo and picnics, which I thought not wise because of so much exposure to other children's germs. Ed went on the field trip, but I stayed behind at the hotel. The climbing wore me out, and I had not yet recovered from jet lag.

Elizabeth had suggested that we take a side trip to Thailand. It was only a two hour flight. Ed and I thought that was a great idea. Before we left Columbus, Elizabeth gave us a list suggesting where to stay, where to eat and her preferences of what to see in Bangkok. I could hardly wait. I told her I loved the music, play and film of *The King and I*, based on an original book, *Anna and The King of Siam*.

"Don't mention that movie, play or music from it, and don't ask anyone about it when you are in Bangkok or around anyone from Thailand," she demanded sternly.

"Why?"

"They think that story reflects badly on their history. Don't ask anyone about it or talk about it or hum any of the songs from that show. You could be arrested."

I thought she was kidding. I started to sing "Getting to Know You" and "Whistle a Happy Tune," both from *The King and I*. Elizabeth glared at me.

§

I didn't feel well the whole time we were in Hong Kong. I felt better in Thailand where we went for three days on our own. The flight was short and the sights, food and people we met were delightful. It was only when we touched down at the airport on the return to Hong Kong that I began to feel seriously ill with flu-like symptoms.

Two days before we were to leave for home, I decided to

call Dr. Lau Chu Pak, Dr. Hummel's colleague. The thought of having a fever and sore throat on a twelve hour flight in a crowded plane made me afraid for myself and the people breathing the same capsuled air. Ed upgraded us to economy plus status, which gave us three additional inches of leg room. Three inches!

Dr. Lau Chu Pak's office was one train stop from our hotel. I had called his office for an appointment and when I told him that I was Dr. Hummel's patient from Columbus, Ohio, he agreed to see me at the end of his day, at five o'clock. His clinic was on an upper floor in a modern office building where high-end shops like Louis Vuitton and Chanel occupied the ground floor.

The small set of rooms where patients were examined was behind a comfortable and compact waiting area filled with locals. They stared at Ed and me. A voice from a cubicle behind a sliding glass window barked orders in the language I didn't understand even from its inflections. I had been surprised that more people in Hong Kong didn't speak English, knowing that not that long ago it was British. Now we heard mostly Mandarin or Cantonese, but I couldn't tell the difference. I was, however, registered by one of the nurses speaking English who told me to sit down and the doctor would see me soon.

I noticed that most of the older patients, both men and women, were accompanied by a younger family member. In

China aging parents are usually cared for by family, not in an assisted living facility.

Newly arrived patients had to register. A few moments later a nurse would call out from behind the glass window for one of the patients to get on the scale against the wall midway down one side of the waiting area. Another nurse checked the patient's weight and shouted it to the nurse behind the window.

Oh no, I thought. Never has my weight been uttered out loud. It's an unspoken number known only to me. Shouting it to all who could hear the not-so-soft voice behind the sliding glass window would be embarrassing. I could not allow it, but I had no choice. Fortunately the Chinese use the metric system and pounds translate to kilograms. My 140 plus pounds translate into roughly sixty-five kilos, a number shouted into the stillness of the waiting room. Didn't sound so bad, but I was easily thirty pounds heavier than anyone else.

Dr. Lau Chu Pak was thorough. He took an EKG and checked my pacemaker. I had not been in A-Fib. Currently I had a fever and other flu symptoms. Checking my list of medications, he dismissed me with a purse full of meds that he dispensed and charged for right there in his office along with the bill. They didn't honor Medicare or any insurance from the U.S.A. They wanted cash. Hong Kong cash. Ed went downstairs and out of the building to find an ATM machine, coming back with the equivalent of $250, the cost for office visit and meds.

The medications included an antibiotic for five days, pain medication and an eight-ounce bottle of deep yellow liquid cough syrup, none of which I used. Sleep was better than anything else.

I could have cried when we boarded the United Airlines flight to Chicago. I was so happy to be going home. I didn't even mind going through security twice—once regular security and again on the Jetway before entering the plane. Sitting in a middle seat didn't upset me. After all, our row had three extra inches of leg room.

Twelve hours later in Chicago we had to go through security again. Finally settled in for the forty-five minute flight home to Columbus, I went digging in my purse for a mint. Wait. What's this? My hand found an unfamiliar oblong object. I had forgotten to remove the eight-ounce bottle of lemon yellow cough syrup that I had dumped into my purse at the doctor's office. It had gone through three security checks undetected.

I stuck the cough medicine in my bathroom cabinet. A year later, when I had a cold, I drank it. The cough went away.

CHAPTER TWENTY
2009-2012

A medical touchdown.

It had been two years since my ablation; eighteen months since beginning the sotalol medication. No A-Fib had showed up on my pacemaker during the last year and a half. Even so, I was taking my pulse twice a day.

Dr. Hummel was pleased. I was thrilled.

"Since the sotalol has worked this long, is it likely that it will continue?" I asked during my annual checkup at the Ross. "Or, will I build up an immunity to it?"

"It appears to be working and will probably continue, but we'll stay with the medication checks every six months for now."

The next question had to be phrased correctly, not blurted out like I was over-anxious.

"Can I go off of the warfarin now?" So much for subtle phrasing.

Dr. Hummel was standing. I was sitting on the edge of the examining table. I saw the look he gave me…like his daughter had just asked to go on her first date.

His right hand crossed in front of his body, his left at a right angle holding up his chin. He drummed his fingers on his face, pacing the short length of the room back and forth for almost a minute before he spoke.

"I'd like to schedule an echocardiogram to find out what adjustments need to be made, if any, before we stop the warfarin. I'm still uncomfortable with you not having the protection of a blood thinner."

"I've been on warfarin for so many years," I said. "Will my body go into shock when I go off of it? Do I need to withdraw slowly?"

"No," he answered. "We'll make the appointment today for the echo, take blood and schedule another appointment. Christine will call you to come in when we get the test results."

Mid-July, 2009, I was back at the Ross. Dr. Hummel charged into the examining room. He was holding the results of the EKG and pacemaker check I had just taken. I could tell he was in a good mood from his smile and twinkling eyes. He sat down at the computer and pulled up my electronic chart containing the recent echocardiogram results.

"Everything looks good," he said. "Again, no A-Fib shows up. We'll stop the warfarin effective today, but I want you to have a full pacemaker check here every three months, not at an OSU Medical Center subsidiary. Here, only at the Ross. No more telephone transmissions. Keep monitoring your pulse daily.

"One more thing," he said as I started to jump off the examining table. "There is no evidence of prior myocardial injury from your heart attack in 2000."

"What does that mean?" I asked, thinking that maybe I really didn't have a heart attack.

"It means that you've had a reversal of functionality from the heart damage. Your heart has repaired itself."

"Is that possible?"

"It's rare," Dr. Hummel said.

I recalled the number of times in the nine years since my heart attack that I was told to be cautious, because heart muscle damage reduces blood flow to the heart.

During the fall a few years ago, there was a shortage of flu shots for everyone during the early weeks of flu-shot season. It was announced that the elderly over age sixty-five, people with heart problems, children and pregnant women would be eligible for vaccination first. I fit into two of those categories: over sixty-five and heart damage from a heart attack.

I just naturally assumed that heart attack damage was permanent, and there was nothing I could do about it. Eating a healthy diet is something I've always done anyway. I am a lifetime Weight Watchers member. It's part of my life, and now if I don't eat that way, I feel terrible. The bad food that has become part of the unhealthy American diet gives me digestive problems, and fat is intolerable because I have no gall bladder.

Exercise has become more and more important. It's not vanity. That's the reason I get up easily three or four mornings a week. And, hanging around forty and fifty year olds who exercise makes my life worthwhile. All are good reasons, but to reverse heart damage, that's the extra point after the touchdown.

§

A few months later I was scheduled for my routine appointment with Dr. Cataland to check thyroid activity. As my primary care physician and endocrinologist, he receives all updated medical information from each one of my doctors.

His first words to me were, "I see that you've reversed all damage from the heart attack you had in 2000."

Two months after that I had my annual appointment with cardiologist Dr. Subha Raman. She always read the chart and test information before she saw me in the examining room. As she walked in, she, too, commented about the information on my chart. "Congratulations. I see you have reversed the function of your heart muscle since your myocardial muscle tissue injury."

"How do you think that happened?" I asked.

"I think you received the best medication possible—exercise and a proper heart-healthy diet."

Isn't that amazing, I thought to myself. I suffered a heart attack in Omaha, Nebraska, all those years ago while giving a sales pitch about heart-healthy foods. I ate healthy then too. Must be genetics and exercise. Maybe I didn't know as much about my own body as I thought I did.

"Are you getting regular eye checkups from your ophthalmologist?" Dr. Raman asked.

"Yes. I just saw Dr. McHale a month ago. I go every six to nine months since my cataracts were removed. Why do you ask?"

"Retinal arteries may become blocked from fat deposits and blood clots like arteries in the heart or neck, especially if there is hardening of the arteries in the eye."

"How would I know I have that problem?" I asked.

"If you get regular eye checks, your doctor will know. If you have carotid artery disease, diabetes, atrial fibrillation, heart valve problems or high blood pressure, you may be a candidate for retinal artery occlusion."

"How does a patient correct it, if she does have it?"

"Retinal artery occlusion is treated like you are treating your heart: statin medication, heart-healthy diet, exercise, regular checkups. If part of the retina artery is blocked and will not receive enough blood and oxygen, you could lose part of your vision."

This was all news to me. Like Gilda Radnor from NBC's *Saturday Night Live* used to say as one of the characters from Weekend Update, "It's always something."

I decided that I must learn about what goes on under my skin. I wasn't sure I knew where all the organs were in relationship to my bone structure. Paul the trainer had a skeletal chart of a human body on the back of a door that faced one of the treadmills at the gym. It also labeled the muscles. It's embarrassing to face up to how little I knew.

Online I clicked on a skeletal poster showing arrows pointing to bones and naming them. The only ones I knew were ribs, skull and pelvis. I recognized tibia and femur and a few others, but I'd never be able to fill them in on a diagram. The muscle chart was even more difficult. There were so many, but I knew that from the soreness I felt after a good workout.

I had to know more if I wanted to be active and not depend on anyone to take care of me. Now, in my seventies, I know that I am repairable, and that maintaining my healthy lifestyle is key to independence and longevity.

I spent days at my computer getting information about my heart, history of problems, medications and terminology. So much information, and so many contradictions. Updates on information are constant. Sometimes old obsolete information isn't deleted even though it's placed next to new data. What to believe?

First I had to find out what happens to the heart after a heart attack, also known as a myocardial injury. *The Free Dictionary* (medical-dictionary.thefreedictionary.com) defines a myocardial infarction as the death of cells in an area of the heart muscle (myocardium) as a result of oxygen deprivation, which is caused by obstruction of the blood supply; commonly referred to as a "heart attack."

The ejection fraction is an important measurement of how well the heart is pumping out blood. The ejection fraction is the total amount of blood in the left ventricle that is pushed out with each heartbeat. A normal ejection fraction reading is between fifty-five and seventy percent. I wanted to know mine.

So, I called Dr. Raman to ask how I could find out the

details of my heart attack: ejection fraction, causes and repair. How do they relate to years of atrial fibrillation? They don't, as far as I could see.

"The most widely used test is the echocardiogram," she said. "I can have my assistant, Cheryl, send you copies of echo test results. How far back do you want to go?"

"My heart attack was in 2000. If possible, I'd like to see anything before that and between the heart attack and my ablation in 2007. Will I be able to understand what I'm seeing?"

"There will be median numbers that you will probably understand."

I thanked her and decided that whatever I received could lead me to ask further questions about specific things.

The packet contained test results from four echocardiograms. I called Medical Records at the hospital for further assistance. An actual person answered. She had a kind and helpful voice. She asked for my name and birth date, and within seconds she had my records.

"What can I help you with?" she asked.

"I'd like to have my medical heart records from 1990 to present," I said.

"I only have records available from the year 2000," she said.

"OK, how can I get them?"

She explained that I could come to the medical records office in the main hospital building. She went on to tell me where and times of availability. I went as soon as I hung up the phone.

Easy. Ninety-six pages, and that was just the heart. There was no charge for the medical records. I took them home to peruse.

The best parts of the reports are the written opinions about doctor/patient dialogues after each visit, or the inter-office communications. If doctors realized how these exchanges of information impact their patients, we might not need so many prescriptions. My interest followed some one-liners (or more) made by my doctors in 2008 and up to present time:

In 2008 after my heart ablation Dr. Caldwell said, *"No current chest pain or atrial fib. Positive for heartburn. Negative for depression."*

In September 2009 Dr. Subha Raman writes, *"I had the pleasure of seeing Rosalie Ungar. She comes to establish with a new general cardiologist after Dr. Caldwell retires."* She goes on to capsule my entire heart history in six and a half lines including, *"She also has a history of CAD presenting with MI while giving a speech on heart-healthy foods in Nebraska."*

In 2014 Dr. Raman writes in her progress notes, *"Thank you for the opportunity to participate in the care of Rosalie Ungar. I look forward to seeing her again in 12 months or sooner as needed. She wrote a memoir that was recently published about her life in France in her 30s working as an au pair, and is looking forward to traveling to France this year as part of book promotion."*

Dr. John Hummel writes in 2015 regarding patient assessment and plan, *"Continue current treatment, long discussion regarding systemic anticoagulation and declines."*

I learned that my ejection fraction since 2007 has been between fifty-five and seventy at each check and that my myocardial injury (heart attack) shows no damage to my heart. Good confirmations on both accounts.

What's next? The anticipation of facing another medical option to manage an incurable condition takes more bandwidth than I have. There's so much to know and so much to do to keep the body going.

What's my blood type? I never even thought about asking that question. Survival is a lot of work. The answer is O positive.

I'm going to have a glass of wine.

CHAPTER TWENTY-ONE
2013

Paul the trainer was moving on. He was organizing a rugby team. He had hopes of being approved to compete in the International Summer Olympics.

Jim Rullo was working on getting his certification as a personal trainer. He trained in other gyms and sometimes joined our morning group to do circuits. I watched in awe. Jim was dedicated and good, yet he wasn't that young…mid-forties, tall and good looking, not as bulked up as many trainers are. He looked normal.

Jim had just left the corporate pharmaceutical world, not sure he'd be able to make it doing what he wanted to do—manage his own gym and workout facility. Timing is everything.

Jim passed his certification with a perfect score. Paul's leaving opened up the smaller-than-average workout space for Jim to remodel. Many of the established clients stayed, as I did. It wasn't long until word got around and more people sought him out.

Personal training saved my life. If I hadn't had a trainer but just a fitness membership at a gym, it wouldn't be the same. For Ed, though, it works differently. He does his own routine in the lower level of our home. I'm not as disciplined. I like and need the social comradery of a group.

Having a definite time to exercise with the trainer gives order to my life. It's part of a schedule, and I do like the harmony that accompanies scheduling. Jim offers flexibility on training times. Classes are around forty-five minutes, usually a little longer if we stay for an extended cool down or cardio extension.

Jim is the reason for his own success. He has a big personality. Knowing Jim is to know everything about him. He's part of our lives, and he cares. In my case, because I'm so much older than the rest of his clients, he modifies some of the exercises while everyone around me is doing something else. For example, because I have two artificial hips, it's not a good idea for me to jump in an exercise and land on my feet or pound my legs like doing jumping jacks. I do squats instead. If something is not injurious, I may want to try while he monitors my moves. Planks and pushups are important, and I can do both with supervision. Jim is quick to praise. He is the best coach I've ever had, even though he sometimes sounds like a Marine drill sergeant.

Along with aging comes less than perfect balance. That's another cautionary move that Jim and his assistant Kevin observe, working on improving my balance while watching that I don't misstep.

My greatest single achievement has come while working on balance: getting up from a lying or sitting position on the floor to a full upright standing position without assistance or holding on. This has helped my golf game too. Preparing to putt the ball on the green, I can actually crouch all the way down sitting on my heels to line up the ball with the hole, then get up from that position without help.

On Sundays Ed and I play golf. We play eighteen holes. It takes about four and a half hours. I count that as a workout and a half, summer only.

A personal trainer is not as costly as one may think. It's less than most prescriptions and in some cases less than the co-pay. Definitely less costly than a heart attack.

§

As stated earlier, I am not a doctor. My theories are my own when it comes to exercise. I have read that muscle mass deteriorates with age. Though I'm not exactly sure at which age, I think that in my late seventies, while my muscle mass is deteriorating, I'm still trying to build more. It's like building a bridge from both sides of the river. At what point do the two sides meet? Keep exercising until the bridge meets or one side may fall down.

In celebration of my seventy-seventh birthday, trainer Jim had everyone who worked out with him that day do a set routine of circuit exercises. We did a total of seventy-seven reps of ten or twelve different exercises. Between each circuit we did cardio either on the treadmill, stationary spinning bike, and rowing machine or elliptical trainer. Circuits included squats, goblet squats, pushups, planks, step-ups, sit-ups, scissor kicks, flutter kicks, reverse and side lunges, crunches, front, lateral and overhead lifts with weights. I use five- or six-pound weights. Everyone else uses heavier ones.

Dr. Thomas Best is Medical Director of The Ohio State University Wexner Medical Center's Health and Fitness Center in New Albany, Ohio. Among a long list of credentials, he also served as a reviewer for the most recent federal guidelines using physical activity. In a recent article for *Healthy New Albany* magazine titled "Movement: The Best Medicine," Dr. Best says in his interview, "With almost every medical problem, exercise has been shown to be as effective as, if not superior to, prescription medications. Exercise is the most powerful medicine we can prescribe for our patients."

"Sometimes," he says, "a little movement is even better than a prescribed remedy. Some exercise is better than none."

I take this to mean that to obsess about exercise is not necessary. I've been doing some exercise/movement for a long time. There have been periods when I've done very little or none. Being consistent is important. Consistency is the way to make exercise a habit. Walking was my habit for twenty years. Now it's strength training and weights along with walking and other forms of cardio. Everyone has to find her own niche.

CHAPTER TWENTY-TWO
2014

Pay attention. Now, that's a phrase to live by. It sums up everything that has to do with the here and now. Like the little black dress, it covers all occasions.

I use it in a physical sense, getting out of the car, walking on an icy sidewalk, keeping one eye on where I'm going while the other eye concentrates on keeping the body balanced. I silently repeat "pay attention and take nothing for granted" so often that the phrase has become my mantra. While growing up, Mother would say, "You have two ears and one mouth, which means you should listen twice as much as you talk."

So, when Dr. John Hummel, head of clinical electrophysiology for Wexner Medical Center at The Ohio State University and the person in charge of my good heart health, consulted with me during an annual appointment, I listened with both ears and paid attention.

Listening also gives one the privilege to challenge what is being said. Besides, four ears were listening. Ed accompanied me to this appointment, as always.

"Your EKG and pacemaker checks are excellent," Dr. Hummel said. "Last stress test results were good. How do you feel?"

"I feel great," I answered. "Best I've felt in twenty years. Except on the days I work out or have a full schedule, I need a nap in the afternoon. But then I am seventy-six."

"Yes," he said. "That's what I want to talk about. Now, don't take what I'm about to say as life threatening or scary. However, after consultations and further checking of test results and recent episodes of chest pain that are thought to be digestive, I need to discuss statistics. You've not had any atrial fib for several years, but that doesn't mean you won't, especially after the age of seventy-five."

He went on talking as he made pencil marks on the back of the EKG report. "We go by a point system to determine what precautions to take as aging occurs. We add one point if over age sixty-five, but two points over seventy-five. If a patient has complications like diabetes or congestive heart failure or smokes, more points are added. One point is added for women. Four points usually mean that precautionary measures should be taken. You have three: you are over seventy-five and a woman."

"Gender and age discrimination," I said. "That's pretty amazing since for years it was the other way around. Women weren't thought to have heart problems and were not treated for such. Only men were taken seriously and most research was done for men, not women. Now women are at more risk?" I asked, not expecting an answer.

Dr. Hummel continued, "To be absolutely safe against a stroke, I'd like to put you back on a blood thinner."

Here's where the "pay attention" comes in and is followed by challenge, negotiation and finally compromise. I was very alert and in a fighting mood, careful not to whine.

"But Dr. Hummel, I only have three points and you said that precautionary methods should be taken at four. Besides, can you consider that I exercise, eat right and that my numbers are excellent? LDL is seventy, HDL is fifty-eight, blood pressure is one hundred twenty over sixty-four, pacemaker keeps me at seventy beats per minute and I haven't had any atrial fib for years. This is my second pacemaker and it still has battery life for three more years. I was on a blood thinner for twelve years and I don't want to go back on it. I take a full aspirin of three hundred and twenty-five milligrams every day. Isn't that enough? Don't the risks of bleeding with a blood thinner out-weigh the good things I've got going?"

"The aspirin doesn't do everything to protect you from stroke," Dr. Hummel said. "When you were on warfarin, there were few blood thinner choices available. Now there are more and they offer a variety of remedies depending on specific problems dealing with blood flow. Some don't need constant monitoring like you had with warfarin, and some can be mon-itored internally with devices similar to your pacemaker or attachments to your pacemaker. So much progress has been made that in the near future it is likely that your heart devices will be transmitted by the WIFI in your home and downloaded to an outside tracking station for monitoring."

Dr. Hummel stopped talking and I could see that he was deep in thought. I had seen this look before when I had been free from atrial fib for a year after my heart ablation and the conversation about stopping warfarin took place. We were in the same kind of examining room at the Ross Heart Hospital when Dr. Hummel made the difficult decision to take me off the warfarin and I felt free—free from bruising, bi-monthly trips to the labs for INR tests, free to eat as many green vegetables as I wanted, shaving my legs without fear of nicking myself.

"I'll tell you what," he finally said as he looked directly at me with a hint of amusement in his eyes. "Would you feel the atrial fib when it occurs if it happens?"

"I don't know. It's been so long since I've had it, but I do take my pulse every day," I said.

"I'll write a prescription for a blood thinner that is fast acting. I won't date it. You carry it with you at all times so that you can get it filled on a moment's notice wherever you are. I want you to take your pulse twice a day. If you go into atrial fib, get the prescription filled and start the medication right away. Then call this office. I'm sometimes hard to track down, but talk to Christine or one of the staff, explain what has happened and we will get you in here quickly. The prescription is for a week, taking one pill twice a day."

"What if I'm only in A-Fib for a couple of seconds or a minute or twenty minutes?" I asked.

"Good question," he said. He talked as we walked out of the examining room giving his notes to those at the scheduling desk to complete my paperwork and instructions. He quickly scribbled the prescription for apixaban.

"Let's make it six to twelve hours in A-Fib before starting the apixaban unless you are short of breath and uncomfortable." He slapped the counter in a rhythm I recognized as atrial fib. "Like this," he said. "And, I want you to come in every three months for a full pacemaker check."

I was getting these checks every six months now. If I had an interim appointment with pharmacology or an appointment with cardiologist Dr. Raman, the pacemaker was checked and an EKG was taken then too.

It's been more than thirty years since I couldn't find my pulse that first time in an exercise class in Louisville. Was I scared then? Am I scared now? The answer is no. I've learned more about my own body than I ever wanted to know. I still can't watch myself or anyone else getting a shot or a needle going into an arm to draw blood or put in an IV. I like to feel good and will do whatever it takes to make that happen.

In the early years of dealing with A-Fib, I asked the doctors if this was genetic. Most didn't think so but they didn't know. Studies were being done. Since that time, my sister, my niece and several of my cousins go in and out of atrial fib. None have died from it.

CHAPTER TWENTY-THREE
2015

Many pacemaker candidates are under the impression that the pacemaker device slows down and speeds up the heart rate as needed. I, too, thought that. Before my first pacemaker implant, when I heard that it would be set at sixty beats per minute, I thought that the device would adjust automatically, slowing the A-Fib down if I went higher than the sixty. Sometimes the A-Fib caused a rate of more than 200 beats per minute, then could go into a different rhythm known as atrial flutter causing my rate to go even higher. When I became the recipient of my first pacemaker in 1999, I learned that the setting at sixty beats per minute would keep me at sixty only if my own heart rate went lower than that; it did nothing if the heart rate went higher.

To ensure I was accurate and specific about this issue, I recently met with Dr. Charles Love, the pacemaker electrophysiologist who initially programed my device. Early in the discussions with him, he answered my questions by drawing a diagram of the heart on the back of a scrap of paper. We were sitting at a Starbucks in Columbus while I interviewed him.

At that time he was still at The OSU Medical Center's Ross Heart Hospital. Since then, he has moved on to New York University as Professor of Medicine and Director of Cardiac Rhythm Device Services.

"Pacemakers come in a number of different forms. The most common one is the dual chamber pacemaker," he said, looking up at me from stirring his coffee. "This device has a wire in the right atrium and one in the right ventricle," he went on to say as he sketched the four parts of the heart labeling the right atrium on top of the right ventricle. "The wire in the atrium assures that the atrial rate does not drop below the rate that is programmed." He paused, taking a sip of coffee, then continued the rough drawing. "Once the patient's own rate drops to sixty, the pacemaker delivers a pacing stimulus as needed to prevent the rate from dropping any lower."

"What happens to the pacemaker while I'm walking fast on the treadmill or exercising?" I asked.

"Most pacemakers can respond to a person's activities

so that the minimum pacing rate will increase as a person walks or runs, thus imitating a normal heart rate response to the exercise."

The more he talked about his specialty, the more excited he got. His eyes widened above his glasses as he drained the Starbucks paper cup. He pointed to his penciled diagram and added a small loop on the side of the left atrium, then tiny circles inside that looked like a mini-tic-tac-toe board. I supposed that was the pacemaker.

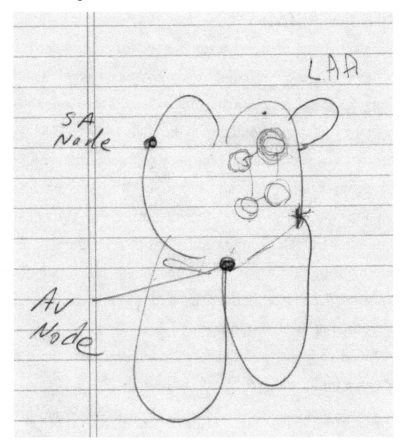

Then, he added a dot in the other atrium, writing the letters "SA Node," and another dot in the middle where the left and right atria meet the left and right ventricles. He labeled that as the "AV Node" connecting it to the edge of the left atrium.

Dr. Love went on to explain, "The pacemaker also assures that once the atria are stimulated, the ventricles beat on time. If they do not follow the lead of the atria, the pacemaker can then deliver a pacing stimulus to the ventricle to keep the atria and ventricles beating in a synchronous manner like a normal heart."

My second pacemaker was installed in 2008. It's checked every three months at the Ross Pacemaker Clinic in a room with computer equipment and a chair that reclines. The electrophysiology technician attaches EKG electrodes onto each arm and my ankles. A "wand," which is really an antenna to communicate with the pacemaker, is placed on my chest. The computer programmer then interrogates the pacemaker which spits out charts, graphs and numbers. The information not only includes how my pacemaker is set and how it's functioning, but it also has information about my heart rates and rhythms. Most importantly, how often I have A-Fib, and how long my heart stays in A-Fib.

During the test, the tech slows down the pacemaker to find the low spot where my own heartbeat kicks in and my heart stops needing to be paced. Even as far back as 2011 this evaluation showed that my atrium is being paced ninety-nine percent of the time. It revealed that my own rate could go as low as thirty-six beats per minute. If the tech had checked how low it actually was, I would have become light-headed and dizzy. After completing the testing, any needed adjustments can be made to the pacemaker through the programmer and the wand.

At the end of each appointment, the scheduler gives me a list of future appointments, what was accomplished, by whom, and a printout of the settings for my pacemaker. I put information about medications and pacemaker checks into my wallet or install as an app on my phone in case of accident, stroke, or incapacitation.

It satisfies me to know that my pacemaker, now set at seventy beats per minute, is on in the atrium all of the time. Its brand name is St. Jude 5826 Zephyr XL DR. I also have its serial number. The lead wires are original and were attached in 1999. The atrial lead is made by Medtronic, while the ventricular lead is made by St. Jude. The most important information I receive during these checks is whether I had any atrial fibrillation since the previous checkup. With the exception of one to five seconds a few times in the last few years, I've been A-Fib free for seven years.

One of the equally important features of the modern

pacemaker is its memory. At a recent clinic check, I asked the technician a question about the three recordings when one to five seconds of atrial fib had occurred. The episodes happened more than a year prior to my request. The technician checked the pacemaker's computer and reported the information. By noting the days of the week and time of day, I was able to recall that all three episodes occurred at the beginning of a workout session when I began a treadmill warm up. A second or five seconds of A-Fib could happen to anyone starting a workout. But it was sporadic, in my case. It does not suggest that I stop using the treadmill.

My niece Lisa also suffered with atrial fibrillation. She has not had a heart attack, and she doesn't need a pacemaker. She had an ablation in January 2014, and she, too, is a patient of electrophysiologist Dr. John Hummel. Presently she does not take an anti-arrhythmia medication or blood thinner, but she does wear a loop recording device under her skin where a pacemaker would be placed. It records any heart arrhythmia she might have, though she's had only one episode since her ablation, shortly after the procedure was completed. Lisa uploads the information on her loop once a month. If she feels that she is in A-Fib, she contacts the electrophysiology department at the Ross.

At my last pacemaker check a few weeks ago, I was given,

as always, an evaluation summary of findings as follows:

"Partial evaluations of the pacemaker shows that sensing thresholds are appropriate. No atrial fibrillation has been recorded. The capture thresholds were stable when last checked. The battery should have approximately two years of service remaining. Programming changes made: none."

I hardly feel my pacemaker unless I put my hand at its location, just under the skin. I can see the small bulge in the upper left chest about halfway between my upper arm and neck and about four inches down from the top of the shoulder. Sometimes, if I don't stand up straight, it's more noticeable. Yet, it's only obvious when I'm wearing a bathing suit or halter workout clothes. I don't mind. I refer to it as evidence of living.

CHAPTER TWENTY-FOUR

2015

My next birthday puts just one year between me and eighty. With the exception of suffering retirees' fixed income blues and watching pharmaceutical and insurance companies double and triple senior drug and co-pay costs, I feel terrific.

Preventive care becomes even more important as these costs go up, and taking care of the body becomes a full time job. Now, however, the cost of a personal trainer has become less than practically all of my co-pays, and certainly less than the prescription costs, even though I have, what I thought was, more than adequate prescription insurance. So, at my annual appointment with Cardiac Electrophysiologist Dr. John Hummel, I had my thoughts laid out when he brought up the subject of blood thinners, again.

Ed and I had been waiting in the examining room at the Ross for less than twenty minutes when Dr. Hummel came in with the pacemaker stats and EKG printout that had been taken less than an hour ago. They were tucked under his arm. He sat down in front of the room's computer pulling the arm of the adjustable system to a comfortable position, typed in the proper info to pull up the rest of my medical information, turned to me and asked, "How's the book coming along?"

"Good," I said. "Almost done. Won't be long until it'll be ready for you to read. Will you write a blurb about it to go on the inside or the back cover?"

"Sure." Changing the subject, he asked, "How do you feel?"

"Better even than last year, especially after a twenty-minute nap sometime between three thirty and four thirty most afternoons."

"You've lost more weight. Are you still working out?" he asked.

"Yes, but I can't eat what I used to and don't have the interest in food that I once had. I do get hungry even though I fill up faster. Just a taste of something is satisfying, whereas before, it wasn't enough. I'm more aware of eating healthy foods in small amounts and not getting full on empty calories.

"I've studied what foods make me feel better and at what times of day I should eat small amounts. Going to bed on a full stomach is the worst. I can't sleep if that happens. Now I've discovered that a good night's sleep is as good as nourishment or medications. That and the exercise," I said.

"Do you do much cardio?"

"We do cardio mixed in with weights. I'm in a small class of men and women all younger than I am. The trainer focuses on core development but tailors certain exercises for me watching that I don't get hurt."

Dr. Hummel scrolled down the computer screen. "It's been a year since you've had any episodes of A-Fib. I see that you requested a copy of your medical heart records from the Records Department."

"Yes," I said. "I needed to see results of various tests showing that I had reversed heart damage from the heart attack in 2000. I especially liked reading comments from doctors and caregivers in inter-office communications. It's all for my book."

"Let's talk about blood thinners," he said.

I knew it.

"You're seventy-eight and a woman. Even though you haven't had any significant A-Fib for eight years, you are a candidate for a stroke."

"I'm still carrying around the prescription for apixaban in

my wallet. You gave it to me last year when we had this discussion. I think it's expired.

"I've done my research on that drug," I said, "and I had twelve years' experience with warfarin. Taking a blood thinner as a preventive doesn't make sense to me, especially when I weigh the pros and cons of taking it. I realize that eight years without A-Fib after experiencing it for thirty years isn't an exact criterion. But lifestyle must have some input, plus the fact that I reversed heart damage from two heart attacks mainly because I exercise and eat a healthy diet. And, I maintain good cholesterol numbers."

Seeing that I was going to continue with my objections to a blood thinner, Dr. Hummel scooted the wheeled stool backwards to face me.

"I've read that apixaban is a good drug, but it's still new. Side effects are rare," I said. "I've taken meds before and had the rare side effects—not often considering all that I take. I may have developed pancreatitis from amiodarone that I took for seventeen years. It was described as a rare side effect in a small study. Apixiban has a rare side effect…brain bleed."

Dr. Hummel listened to me calmly but seriously. "Still, as you get older, with your heart history and genetics, you are a stroke candidate."

"I know, but I just think of all the inconveniences of taking a blood thinner. What if I need a different surgery not related to the heart? Then, I'll have to go off the blood thinner for a few days, another risk, and take something in place of it like Lovenox. Yuck.

"I understand that if someone is having a stroke and they call nine-one-one and get to the hospital for treatment within an hour, that the damage from a stroke can be diminished or eliminated. Is that true?"

He spoke leaning forward, "In most cases, yes. Often it can be one to two hours."

"What are the symptoms?" I asked. "Would I recognize a stroke?"

"Yes, the symptoms of a stroke are not subtle. You would know you are stroking."

"Then in almost all cases I could make it to the hospital in time." I didn't wait for his reply, but went on, "I think, Dr. Hummel, that it's up to me if I take the risk either way—stroke or brain bleed. The odds are perhaps the same."

In a low voice almost under his breath, he said, "I wouldn't take it either, if I were you." On a lighter note in a firmer voice he said, "I'll write you another prescription for the apixaban to carry in your wallet. Also, I'll give you a voucher for a free two-week supply good at any pharmacy, if you need it."

I didn't feel good about my victory as I looked at Ed who

observed with interest the conversation between Dr. Hummel and me. I wasn't gloating and wanted both men to know that.

"It's not that I'm anti-medications or even anti-new meds, Dr. Hummel. On the other hand, I've been taking estrogen hormones for over twenty-five years, starting in early meno-pause at a time when most menopausal women were taking hormones unless there was history of cancer in the patient's family. I was fifty-two. A few years later there were studies showing that cancer could be caused by hormone replacement drugs, even though prior studies showed that the same drugs could prevent heart attacks.

"Instead of presenting more than one benefit or side effect of hormone replacement drugs, the FDA and doctors decided that all women should stop taking these drugs even if there was no family cancer, as was my case. I tried to stop but was so unhappy and physically miserable with hot flashes and night sweats, mood swings, forgetting things and sexual disinterest that I begged him to let me continue taking estrogen. I even offered to sign an affidavit accepting all responsibility."

Dr. Hummel stood—appearing to wind up the discussion. Focusing on completing his examination of my heart rhythm and breathing, he said he would see me again in a year.

§

It just so happened that my annual gynecology appointment was scheduled soon after the Dr. Hummel checkup. This would be my second yearly exam with the new gynecologist, a woman.

At our first meeting I found her understanding and easy to talk to. We discussed my gynecological problems and their effects on aging. She said that a little more hormone replacement would fix those problems. I decided not to push it and stay with what I was taking, the smallest dose possible.

When I went back this year, I thought about asking her to start weaning me off hormone replacements altogether. Was my tirade with Dr. Hummel about blood thinners giving me doubts now about hormones?

She suggested that I start going off the hormones slowly. I would start taking them only every other day. Then a week later every three days, and then once a week, and wean off completely after that. The doctor said I might experience some menopausal symptoms but they would probably disappear eventually.

I felt good about ending hormone replacement therapy. As she proceeded with the physical exam, ending with the breast exam, she asked if I examined myself on a regular basis. I don't. She spent extra time checking the left breast. I reminded her that my pacemaker was on that side and that the robotic heart bypass surgery fifteen years before tied off the mammary artery. As a result, the two sides are not identical.

She had a serious look on her face as she pulled the paper gown around the front of my upper body. "I feel a mass on the left side and want you to have a mammogram." I'd had a mammogram last year and wasn't scheduled for another until next year.

She checked my chart for notes from the previous year. "You didn't have an ultrasound on the left side. I don't know why. When can you come in to the Women's Health Clinic?"

The floor under me was giving way. This was the last thing I expected. I couldn't answer her. I wanted her to tell me that it was probably nothing, but that she wanted to be cautious. She didn't say that.

An appointment at the Women's Clinic was made for the following week. I didn't think I could survive a whole week not knowing. What if it is breast cancer? What then? I had been comfortable embracing aging because others were going through it too. I had experienced the heart issues earlier than most and could guide some through it. Breast cancer was another story. I was older than most breast cancer patients. Would Medicare pay for treatments and drugs, or would the younger patients, survivors and health care workers look at me and think, "She's old and going to die soon anyway. Why bother?"

Is this my fault? Should I have ended the hormones years ago? I felt like a smoker who gets lung cancer after years of smoking and being told to quit. Does that smoker get blamed for her own death?

§

The health care technician pulled and tugged and squeezed to get as much tissue in the x-ray as possible. She asked me to wait while she checked the developed tests for visual quality the doctor needed.

I was calm, not nervous. I felt that there was no cancer and probably no mass. The doctor came in smiling. "There's no evidence of anything unusual in your mammogram. It looks exactly the same as the one you had fifteen months ago. No changes," she said. "We'll see you a year from now."

Maybe. I'll stop the hormones: That's one less worry and two fewer prescriptions. Did I assert myself too much with Dr. Hummel? Do I need to adjust my thinking?

No. Keep life simple and own your tomorrow.

CHAPTER TWENTY-FIVE
2016

It's been more than thirty-five years since my first episode of atrial fibrillation. At that time, I didn't know what atrial fibrillation meant. Irregular heartbeat? I didn't know what that meant either. Still, my journey to find out didn't start for another two years and continues on until this day. Time changed everything—my understanding of the doctor's role and my own role in the management of the disease.

Ignore the problems and they'll go away. I knew better. My thyroid problems didn't...ever. Not even now, almost sixty years after their diagnosis.

It used to be the philosophy of many, including me that medical decisions were up to the doctor. Whatever the doctor told us to do, we did. Of course, the life expectancy at that time was many years less than it is now. What's changed? Time, education, communication, technology, medical malpractice insurance and the internet.

Do some doctors understand that we patients don't understand what they are saying most of the time? Are we listening? At first I wasn't. Fix the problem. A pill, an operation? Did I ask questions or say that I didn't understand? No.

My conclusion is that a partnership needs to be formed between doctor and patient. The doctor has had years of education and training. But the patient needs to educate herself about the problem, possible solutions, the positives and negatives surrounding treatment and medications. Keeping up with new information and discoveries is critical. The patient must ask questions and request answers that she will understand. I discovered from my doctors that asking questions until I understand the answers encourages some doctors to open up more and more. I stopped nodding my head that I understood when I didn't.

None of my health issues are cured. They are managed. Things change as we age: wear and tear on joints, digestion and plumbing. As I lose height and weight, medication dosage sometimes has to be adjusted. Appetite fluctuates. Memory is still intact but often I have to pause and reach for the right word.

Exercising the brain is as important as exercising the body. I play bridge, do crossword puzzles, read and make up memory games recalling people's names and items in a group.

Three times a week at the gym with Jim the trainer is part of my social life and physical happiness. A few months before my seventy-ninth birthday, Jim included in the session of circuit training one hundred of each exercise. One hundred push-ups were a problem. I had to stop for ten seconds at fifty before finishing the one hundred.

Getting closer to eighty means adjusting how one thinks about making plans for the future. I've come a long way in understanding myself, my medical management and my doctors. No longer am I afraid to ask questions, ask them again or be afraid that those in charge will think I'm stupid. It doesn't matter. I'm entitled to make suggestions about my own body. I take responsibility for the consequences.

A stress-free day, a glass of fine red wine with a healthy dinner, a good book and a quiet night of uninterrupted sleep provide comforts I never imagined.

Good health is fragile. It takes effort. Is it worth it?

You betcha. In a Heartbeat.

ACKNOWLEDGMENTS

In A Heartbeat: The Ups and Downs of Life with Atrial Fib takes place from 1980–2016. My first memoir, the award-winning *No Sex in St. Tropez*, is a narrative set in 1974 Europe. Both books depended on my recollection of past events and characters. Thanks to a good memory and manageable health issues, I was able to accomplish the writing of two very different memoirs.

Neither could have been written without the help of dedicated people. Some assisted on both as did my BFF and first draft editor, Dr. Joan Simon.

Special thanks go to publisher Brad Pauquette at Boyle & Dalton, a division of Columbus Publishing Lab. His gentle encouragement and authoritative kindness have made me a better editor for my own work. Thanks also to Emily Hitchcock, also of Columbus Publishing Lab, for her expert copy editing.

The physician experts who encouraged the writing of my story from the patient's point of view were generous with their time and information. So, thank you Dr. Charles Love, Dr. John Hummel, Dr. Samuel Cataland, Dr. Subha Raman and Dr. Jeffrey Wasserstrom.

Thank you Howard Seiferas, Peter Dray, Jim Rullo and to the members of Writers Satellite, a critique group meeting and eating pizza on alternate Tuesdays. I thank Rose Ann Kalister, Peg Hanna, Brenda Layman and Francoise Bartram. We are a prolific group of writers who will each publish a book in 2016. Our ages range from fifty-five to seventy-nine.

To my good friends who read advance and in some cases unedited manuscripts, I thank Karen Strip, Mary Elizabeth Doyle, Marilyn Minkin, Ellen Kozberg and Suzanne Kull. My sister Joan Wallick is a strong force that continues to keep me going on a daily basis. I thank all of these wonderful women. They have sold a ton of books for me.

I thank fellow members of the Central Ohio Branch of National League of American Pen Women. It is an honor to be part of NLAPW, a distinguished group of writers and artists.

To my husband, Ed, who reads every word of each draft

before it comes off the computer, I thank him for confirming to me that it's important to have family believe in you.

Of our ten grandchildren that I mentioned by name in acknowledgments of *No Sex in St. Tropez,* four of them are now writing. I'll repeat the advice I gave them before: Live life, then write about it.

Buy Rosalie's books on Amazon or Barnes & Noble or go to Rosalie's website: www.RosalieUngar.com and click on the links to your favorite retailers.

Contact Rosalie at: rosalie@rosalieungar.com